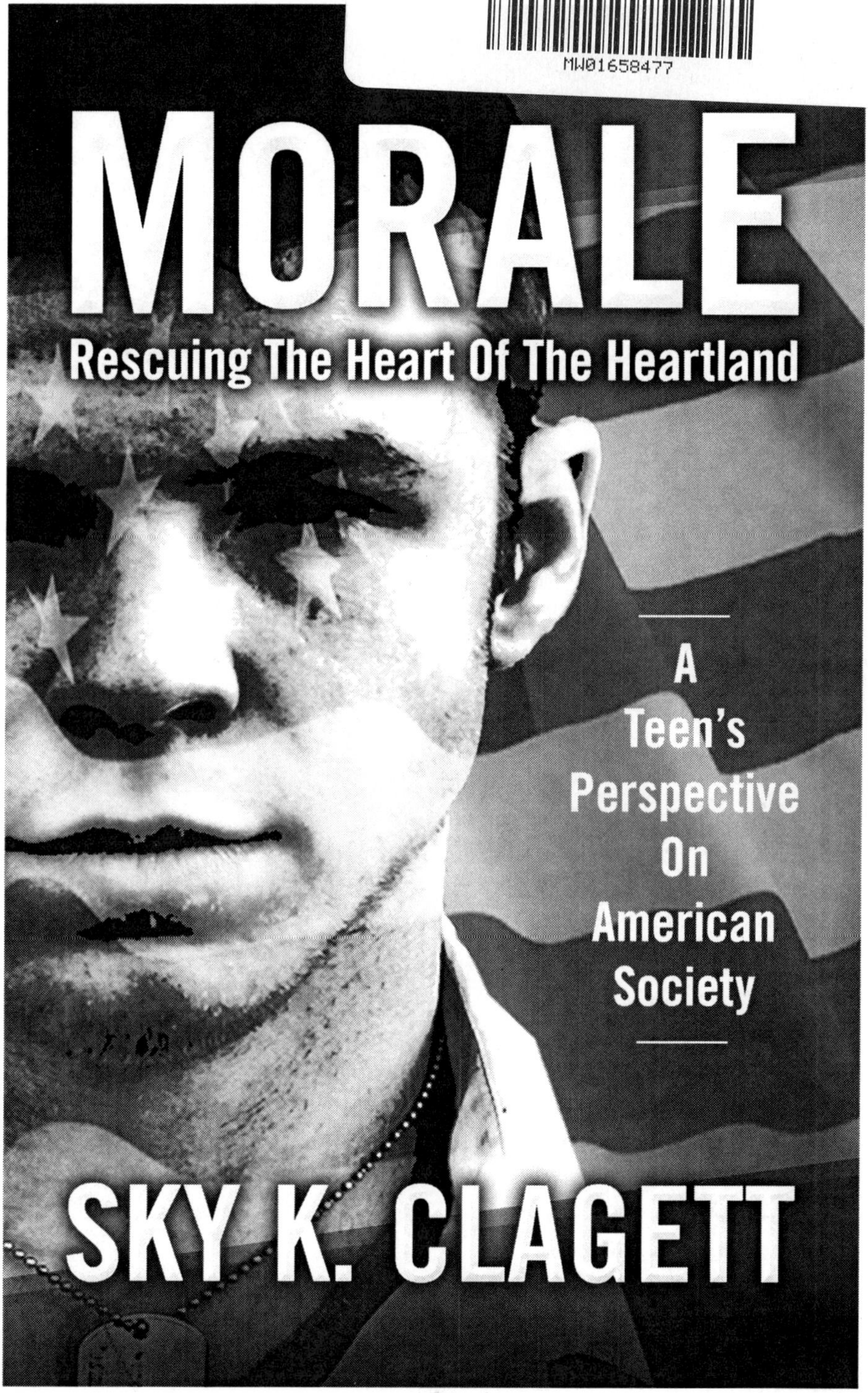
MORALE
Rescuing The Heart Of The Heartland
A Teen's Perspective On American Society
SKY K. CLAGETT

ISBN 978-0-615-50967-9

Printed in the United States of America

Edited by Gary Myers
Cover Design by Sky Clagett & Dustin Myers Design
Interior Layout by Dustin Myers Design

Dedicated to those who didn't compromise when compromising seemed like the only option. It is by their strength in standing, hard work, and God's grace and favor that this Country has made it through the storms it has faced. Because of those who were brave enough to stand for us and those still brave enough today to continue to fight for us, we are and we will remain the single greatest country in the world.

To Pat & Don Harris

You are the answer!

Contents

Acknowledgements

First and foremost, my God, Who I pray has only used me as a vessel to speak His own wisdom onto these pages. He is the one who I know was always there watching over me with love, and with His great plan for my life, though I may not always understand it. He has had His hand on this country since its birth, and it is only by His mercy, faithfulness, and chosen few that this country has survived for as long as it has, and I thank Him for it daily.

To the role models I am proud to call my family; my parents, Joseph and Michelle Clagett and my grandparents, Gary and Florine Penrod. They are not perfect, but each of them has had a hand in raising me into the man I am destined to become, teaching me along the way about principle, values, morals, hard work, integrity, strength, pride, patriotism, and valor. Not one of them has ever shown me anything but support, and they have never played their role in my life selfishly, unlovingly, or contrary to my best interests. They are all heroes to me, and I'm more blessed than I ever could have hoped to be to have been born into this family.

To all of my closest friends, and my siblings who have supported me in everything I have shot to accomplish in my life and who continue to be there for me as I continue to dream. Also to the mentors I have been raised by. I'm blessed to have parents who know how to choose the right friends. Thank you for being God's light in my life. My second grade teacher, Mrs. Kathy Cordes, who pushed and strongly believed in my ability to succeed. Mike & Mary Coate, who taught me the value of faith and true heart-felt charity and love. Walter & Diana Echols, who taught me the importance of family and hard work. Teresa & Ken Ess, who taught me how to hold true to responsibility and dedication. Brian & Sarah Page, who taught me how to keep on the straight and narrow of life and still know how to enjoy it. Shelly Larue, who taught me the strength that comes from living a life of real compassion and self-success. Kent & Tressa Powell who showed me how to keep God's word as a strong-point in my life. Linda & Jerry O'Bryan, who showed me the importance of reverence and respect. Theresa Tucker Saunders, one of the strongest women I have ever had the blessing of having in my life. Sue & Dave Ponzar, who showed me that stewardship should never involve corner-cutting. Don & Shelia Moran, who prayed God's blessing and conviction into my life. Finally, all of my family here at home on the Penrod side, and over in Maryland on the Clagett side. Both have loved me and raised me to be someone who I pray will bring each of them honor and pride.

To the heroes I look up to in my life

My father, Joseph Kenneth Clagett: A man of integrity who has worked dead-end jobs, countless hours, and has been through hell and back to get to the high position he is in today. To me he is the most honorable, faithful man that I have ever had the great fortune of calling MY father. Dad, though I may not always have shown it in my past seventeen years on this earth, I want you to know that I hold a great respect for you, as well as a great pride towards you and that all the wisdom you have taught me is the inspiration behind every word in this book. I love you, dad.

To my Grandfather, Gary Barton Penrod (U.S. Navy, U.S. Army), and my uncle, Gary Kenneth Penrod (U.S. Marines): They are both veterans, and two men that I look to for guidance and support. I am proud to call them both my family, and even more proud to call them my heroes. They both hold a great pride in what they endured in the service, as well as a great pride for this nation, as I do. I honor them both, and will continue to pass the patriotism, honor, and yes, even all the stories, to my family one day. Thank you both. I love you.

To my Senior Pastor, Dr. Timothy Bryan Cutshall: A true man of God in every sense of the word. Many of the references and things in this book have been inspired by his kind, and bold words of wisdom and love. He gives God the credit for everything in His life, and I'm proud to call him my pastor. I pray that God continues to feed him daily and protects him and his family as they continue to grow in their faith and bless others with their compassion. Thank you "Pastor B", for all the wisdom and love you have blessed my family with over the years.

To both of my Youth Ministry Mentors, Christopher & Stephanie Gilbert, and Chris & Amye Quinn: Thank you all for guiding me down the right path and for putting up with me even in my "younger years." As I grow up, I want each of you to know that the man I hope to become, you had a part in shaping and you played your parts very well. I hope that the person I become brings each of you pride. I love all of you very much and my prayer for each of you and your families is that God continues to bring each of you protection, love, and wisdom as you keep spreading His word to kids like me who need it. I pray also that He raises up more people like you, so that future generations have a place of integrity and safety to go to. God bless each of you.

And finally, to all of the Soldiers who are still fighting for us away from home. Thank you for standing up for us when no one else would, and for fighting for our honor, as well as the freedom we so easily take for granted lately. I hope one day soon to be able to join you in fighting America's enemies, both foreign and domestic, for the protection of our families. You deserve nothing but our utmost respect, honor, and prayers. We miss you and pray for your safe return home. God bless you.

To My Great Grandmother,

Arline Elizabeth Jackson

February 4, 1916 - December 7, 2010

Hope you're having fun breaking in your new wings, Grandma J. We love and miss you, and will see you again soon.

Introduction

Merriam-Webster's Dictionary defines the word morale as moral principles, teachings, or conducts and the level of individual psychological well-being based on factors such as a sense of purpose and confidence in the future. Basically, it's the level of confidence one has in the future of something or in "something" itself. Before this book had even become a thought in my head, I had watched the country I love and have grown up in begin a slow decline, not just economically and politically, but also morally. We have begun to lose sight of the foundation of principles and dreams that holds us together, and as someone who has seen what happens when you lose sight of morality or humanity, it scares me.

That's when I decided to make a choice: Am I going to get scared, sit back and say, " I'm just one person, I can't make a difference so I shouldn't even try?" Or will I let this burn deeply enough within me to be able to make a stand for what I believe in? And that is the same self-addressed question that I hope you will have answered for yourself by the time you reach the last page. America and her people have fallen asleep, and while we have been asleep, people who are hungry for nothing but power and self-indulgence have been wide awake, setting up a plan for the destruction of America's original foundation.

This is not just a book about humanity and the human spirit; this is meant to be the draft of a rescue plan - a rescue plan for our suffering republic. Unlike the lies and excuses emanating from Washington that seem to be drawn out and call for the overthrowing of principles, the procedure for THIS rescue plan lies rooted in seven forgotten principles: Enlightenment, peace, truth, integrity, diversity, restoration and common sense. It's time for us to start listening to the alarm clock that is our Constitution, our history, our rights as people and the Word of God before they are taken from us. They have been ringing for too long, and waking up principle, virtue, faith, and common sense is the only thing that will restore the confidence that we have gradually lost in this nation.

You won't find much about politics in this book, and what little you do find is backed completely by fact. The idea behind this is not politics. What this plan is focused on is the restoration of morality and common sense in America. There isn't a lot about debt, interest rates, unnecessary airport security measures, or the juicy gossip behind Barbie and Ken's recent divorce (although, I hear it had something to do with Ken sleeping around with one of those Bratz dolls. It's ok though, I hear Barbie got the dream house).

While issues like those ARE very important and need to be spoken of and looked into, there is one thing that needs to be fixed before we as a country are ready to repair anything economically or politically. That is America's morale, the level of confidence we have in our future. Ask yourself if you're confident about where we are going, or if you even know enough about it to hold an opinion?

I believe the first step in rescuing America, is rescuing America's heart, and what lies inside it along with founding principles; its morale. American philosopher, essayist, and poet George Santayana once stated, "Those who cannot remember the past, are condemned to repeat it." That line has rung true since the dawn of humanity and if we'd just look back through our history, we could see that for ourselves. We need to start remembering where we came from and how we got here, wake up and replant our nation in the freedoms we have so long taken for granted. It is in the principles of the past and pride in where we come from where we will find America's cobwebbed heart.

In these first few pages you may have already formed an opinion of me based on the things I've said. Maybe you believe I'm biased or too young to know what's going on. Let me tell you something about myself. I stand firmly by my belief in God and the vast amount of pride I hold for my country, but I'm not here to push my lifestyle or my own principles on you. What I want is for this book to help you find something to stand for. My prayer is that it will give you back your confidence in our nation. All I am here to do is present the facts, and back EVERYTHING I say with pure fact and what I know is true, as well as what my forefathers deemed necessary in the fight to remain the free, opportunistic land and the heart-rooted nation we have always been known for.

Whether or not you choose to accept the truth I present is up to you, but at the very least, I hope this helps you find something to stand for. When it comes to head-butting opinions, we will always argue and disagree, but in the end we are in this as a united front. When it comes down to it, I couldn't care less where you stand politically. What I really care about and hope that you care about is whether or not you choose to be individuals who, above all political standpoints, root yourselves in honesty and integrity, and want the absolute best, not for yourselves or your crying wallets, but for this nation, your families, and your neighbors. If this is what you represent, then I am proud to stand by you, regardless of what you believe politically. I'm going to get into a lot of things in the next few hundred pages, not just the country, but in humanity, heartache, and courage.

So with that, my deepest hope is that you can look past the writer, and more so at the words you are reading. Let them soak into your heart and then find your voice, as a human being, and as an American. People keep asking each other with all we are facing, "can America still survive?" My answer is "yes." Together, we can change the world. Someone just has to make the first move. Maybe you saw the cover of this book, and wondered why the title was written the way it was: MoralE. It wasn't a typo, it wasn't an accident, and no, I was not trying to emphasize the word ORAL. I wrote it that way because a high morale is a large part of America's success, and America is a nation founded on the ideals of the human spirit. Morale is a starting point, and while we need to be able to band together as a nation in unity, we must first individually make the choice to be people who are willing to stand up for what we believe in. There is no 'I' in team, but there is a 'ME' in morale. The spirit of a nation lies in the hearts of it's people, and before unity can be accomplished for any team, every player has to first find their drive. Together, rallying up, in peace, and through our rights as citizens, we can save the nation. Someone just has to be the one willing to call everyone together.

Regardless of what party you belong to, every American

should have pride for this country. Far too many sacrifices have been made for us to just forget what America stands for, so let's remember where we came from. I hope this brings you enjoyment and enlightenment. Let's rescue the Heart of the Heartland together.

1
The Birth Of Hope

"Our attachment to no nation upon earth should supplant our attachment to liberty."
–Thomas Jefferson

"*We hold these truths to be self-evident, that all men are created equal, that they are endowed by their Creator with certain unalienable Rights that among these are Life, Liberty and the pursuit of Happiness.*" We've all heard these words at some point in our life, and if you haven't … well, you've probably been underneath a rock. These words were part of the document that birthed the United States: The Declaration of Independence.

The birth of the U.S. wasn't just the birth of another country, it was unique. Not only because of how it has affected the course of world history and the growth of democracy, but because everything that the U.S. is built on, and so much of our National history, ties back to this single document. The first, most crucial component in this rescue plan is learning history, knowing history, and remembering how we arrived where we are. You may say it's boring, you may say it's unnecessary, but the fact of the matter is, the less we know, the less we remember, the more likely we are to fail. So what this chapter is all about, is remembering. After all, the best place to start anything is at the beginning.

Without a beginning, you can't have a story or a plan. So I'm starting with history, OUR history. We all know the basic gist; King George III and Great Britain had us tight in their monarchial grip, but we disagreed with their way of Government. That eventually led to the Declaration of Independence, written by Thomas Jefferson, which severed America's - or what back then was known as the "United Colonies" - ties to Great Britain, making us a new country, and democracy. We all get that, and knowing the basics is good, but knowing the details is what makes the story of America's birth so powerful and influential across the world.

We also know that the Declaration of Independence was signed and eventually passed through Congress, which signified the birth of a free country. However, what we tend to forget is that there was so much leading up to just the writing of the first draft of the Declaration, and we've also very steadily but very surely forgotten how much sacrifice was made to pass this document.

Declaring a new country was a decision that the founders did not take lightly. They realized the risk they took in committing treason against the British government. In fact, they had tried everything to avoid any type of hostility, including the "Olive Branch Petition," they had sent to King George III a year earlier on the fifth of July in 1775, requesting his help in the road to peace.

The first Continental Congress had also attempted sending King George III a petition for redress of grievances.

Unfortunately, the King was hot tempered, power hungry, and pretty stubborn (those tight, puffy English 1700's pants will do that to you), and neither received a response. So the Continental Congress began to put into effect the only option they had left: Revolution. A new American currency had been established by June, 1775 which didn't go unnoticed by King George III. In August of 1775, he declared a royal proclamation that us *"American subjects"* were *"engaged in open and avowed rebellion"* (2), which led to the passing of the American Prohibitory Act later that year. That meant that all American cargo and ships belonged to Britain.

But, Congress continued to cut the colonies' ties to the mother country in the process of becoming a new, independent nation. In resistance to Parliament's American Prohibitory Act of 1775, Congress passed the Privateering Resolution in March of 1776, allowing the colonists to *"fit out armed vessels to cruize on the enemies of these United Colonies"*(1). For us, this meant that if Britain messed with our ships overseas, we gave ourselves the right to mess theirs up. Because of this, American ports were able to open commerce with other nations on April 6, 1776, officially severing the economic tie held by the Navigation Acts. The object of these acts was to protect English shipping, and to secure a profit to the home country from the colonies, which meant little profit for us here. So, Thank God for the "who's got the bigger stick" game.

Thomas Paine, son of an English Quaker Artisan father, and Anglican mother had held many jobs before moving to Philadelphia and writing his 47-page work "***Common Sense***," which was said to have sold more than 500,000 copies after being published in February, 1776. Paine's love for America and devotion to the American cause of independence sparked his evolution into a revolutionary writer of argumentative work encouraging opposition to the crown, like his work, "*Crisis Papers.*"

Paine's work sparked the American revolutionary movement within the thirteen colonies. Not long after publication, some of Paine's argument found resounding recollection in the Declaration itself, but we're still not quite there yet ... stay with me just a little longer. On May 10, 1776, a new resolution was passed: The Resolution for the Formation of Local Governments. By the time this came around, we were becoming more and more convinced that independence was certain. By May in 1776, eight of the thirteen colonies had decided to support independence, and on May 15, 1776, the Virginia Convention passed another resolution which stated, *"the delegates appointed to represent this colony in General Congress be instructed to propose to that respectable body to declare the United Colonies free and independent states."* In June of 1776, Congress learned that Great Britain had hired German mercenaries to attack America from the inside. To Great Britain we were, at this point, considered a "*foreign entity*" that had to be dealt with.

In Philadelphia, on June 7, 1776, in a session in Pennsylvania Statehouse (which later became known as Independence Hall) Richard Henry Lee of Virginia read his resolution beginning: *"Resolved: that these United colonies are, and of right ought to be, free and independent states, that they are absolved from all allegiance to the British Crown and that all political connection between them and the State of Great Britain is and ought to be totally dissolved."* Of course, there were still those who leaned more toward reconciliation with Britain. On June 11, consideration of Lee's resolution was postponed by a vote of seven colonies to five without a vote from New York. Congress then took a little break for three weeks. Before recessing, five men were chosen to draft a case for the Colonies' independence.

Among this Committee of Five was Benjamin Franklin of Pennsylvania, Robert R. Livingston of New York (who in the end, never signed the Declaration), Roger Sherman of Connecticut, John Adams of Massachusetts, and of course, Colonial Rock star Thomas Jefferson of Virginia (insert cheesy sitcom applause). Jefferson instantly took upon himself the responsibility of writing a draft of what would soon be known as the United States' Declaration of Independence. When his ink was dry, he presented it first to John Adams and Dr. Benjamin Franklin, who helped Jefferson make a few revisions before the Committee was to present it to Congress.

The Declaration had three stages: Jefferson's original draft, the copy with Adams' and Franklin's revisions, and finally, the one that was eventually adopted. On July 2, 1776, the Lee resolution had been adopted by twelve of the thirteen colonies with New York, again, not voting. New York played the indecisive teenage girl role of the original colonies. The Declaration then went through a revising process.

This process led straight into July 3, and into the early morning of July 4. Contrary to popular belief, only two founders showed up to sign on July 4, including a man named Charles Thomson, who was not present when the rest of the founders reconvened to sign a clean draft a month later. The Declaration wasn't formally signed until August 2. But we celebrate the completion and passing of the document on the fourth of July.

Now, you have to wonder why this process was so strenuous. I can tell you right now, it wasn't because of the politics. In fact, most of the men in congress disagreed on a wide array of issues, but they knew that a successful revolution came from unity. It wasn't at all about what the men of congress found rational or that they worried how the big, scary Parliament would take it. What it was about was the dream. The fight to gain America's independence was by NO means a signed, sealed, delivered deal. The road to the ultimate goal was marked with a vast amount of hardship, and sleepless nights for the men who fought so hard to see it become a reality. History tells us that most of the men who signed their name to this document were demonized, even killed violently in some cases.

Most lost their homes by fire, set by the British. Others lost members of their family, or both their homes and their family. But unlike so many politicians today, the men of 1776, while they feared the outcome, believed that what they were doing was worth the sacrifice. Stephen Hopkins of Rhode Island signed with a shaking hand, yet he boldly stated, *"My hand trembles, but my heart does not."* They didn't bury their head in the sand, and they weren't in it for the looks and fame. They stood firm in their belief and aspiration to one day witness the forming of a more perfect union, and to see the birth of a free land. Or, create the opportunity for future generations to see it.

John Adams once said, *"I am well aware of the toil, and blood, and treasure that it will cost us to maintain this Declaration, and support and defend these states. Yet, through all the gloom, I can see rays of ravishing light and glory. I can see that the end, is worth more than all the means."* They stood united against tyranny because they firmly believed in every human being's right to govern and think for themselves. That under God, anything can be achieved, and that life, liberty, and the pursuit of happiness are CERTAIN rights granted to you the day that you begin life on this earth. They believed in a fair chance for everyone who was willing to work. They believed in the hope and possibility of one Nation that could change the face of the world, and they believed that the government is to be run by the people. Look back into history; you can plainly see just how strongly these men believed in their cause. The first person to sign the Declaration was President of Congress, John Adams. When Adams signed it, he didn't sign it small, somewhere in the corner, he signed it directly under the Declaration's body in a large font.

He wanted his name to stand out because he was unafraid of who saw it. He wanted everyone to know that he backed up this new government 100 percent. People today will say that this country was founded by revolution - and it was - but unlike most revolutions, it wasn't defined by the amount of blood spilt. It was defined by the passion for freedom.

We didn't ask for a war. In fact, most of the colonists were very much opposed to the idea of a war. But in the end, we knew that freedom came with a price, a price we had to be willing to pay for generations to come, even if that meant war. The difference between a revolution founded solely on violence, and the American Revolution was that violently led revolutions occur when a group of people rise up in an effort to radically change one's political system. The American Revolution led by our founding fathers was not based on the idea of radically changing Parliament's rule of law. We wanted our own; we wanted to solely cut ourselves FROM Britain's law, not to change it. Because we believe in controlled government, one in which the people have the chance to think for and govern themselves, and we were very much against the idea of taxation without representation, for which King George III had been infamous. This revolution was a revolution of the hope of a new nation, not violence.

We didn't want violence, but we were more than willing

to do whatever it took to stand up for what we believed in. Patrick Henry said it best: *"I know not what course others may take, but as for me; give me liberty, or give me death."* He also said, *"If this be treason, make the most of it."* Henry wasn't insinuating or promoting violence, but he firmly stood for his freedom, which is more than you can say for today's generation. Ask yourself, are we still that America? The one our founders fought, died, and dreamed for? Are we still a country that is built on freedom and hope, and if so, are we still courageous enough to stand by it? Well, if you think we are, then this certainly isn't the country I've been learning about since I've been in school, but if you see that we aren't, know that we CAN be once again. This attempted reconstruction of our ideals by the radically corrupt of today may feel like it came out of no where, but trust me when I tell you, that it's been a long time coming.

It isn't a specific party's fault; it's taken a little bit from all of us. We've been so focused on the politics of things, that we've literally blinded ourselves to the thieves that have entered from backstage who are slowly taking down the "old sentiment" of freedom, and setting in place a new base of nationalism in which they get the power they are starved for. The signers of the Declaration in 1776 understood that our rights came from God, and that people have the ability to think for and to govern themselves. But today, the imperative truth that we have yet to realize is that until we find as much passion to fight for our freedom and our republic, as the corrupt in power have to take it from us, we will lose this country and everything for which our forefathers fought and died.

This country was just handed down to us, which in turn causes us today to take it much more lightly than it should be, and we have taken it for granted for too long. We need to remember that this country was given to us through great sacrifice. If we want this country to survive, we have to be willing to stand up for it. In 1776, after the Declaration had been signed, Dr. Benjamin Franklin was asked by a bystander what congress had created for the people of the United Colonies. He answered, smiling, *"A republic, if you can keep it."* We can move our train back onto the right track; it IS possible.

All we have to do is wake up, realize what's going on and then make a choice to stand up. The answer to the revival of our nation is not to be left to Washington D.C. The answer lies in the people awakening to the actions and realism of the corrupt, and stopping them the way our founders intended for us. Some may be saying that so much evil and injustice has taken place since America's birth—slavery, terrorism, political changes in the system, communism, wars, and all the inhumane Britney Spears singles— that there couldn't possibly be anything left of the founders' vision that could be compatible with today's survival-of-the-fittest society, or at least not much. I disagree. I believe that it is by remembering that those types of events occurred and learning from them, allowing ourselves to avoid them, that keep our founders' faith and hope alive.

By remembering our history, we are able to remember where we have been and where we have the ability to go. In defense of my forefathers' vision, I solemnly believe that, even if we can't see it now, even if we feel like it's too far gone to get back, like faith, it IS there. We just have to find the courage and strength to awaken the spirit of our root principles and values. The principles and values that the signers of the Declaration and the authors of the Constitution intended; things like freedom, happiness, thrift, honor, integrity, hard work, dreams, hopes, charity, strength and of course, unity.

The British army in 1776, thought we were weak, that we were an untrained, uncompelled, scared group of farmers who had gotten big heads. They thought we were going to be a pushover, an obstacle that was considered more of a workout rather than a fight. They were wrong. They underestimated who we are. Yes, ARE. Not past tense. What they didn't take to mind, was the fact that while we didn't have all the supplies or profit that they had, there was one thing we did have that they lacked: Drive and American perseverance. Today, the progressives and other people in power play the part of the British in 1776. They expect us to do nothing. They believe that their reconstruction will go uninterrupted, but they haven't taken our spirits to mind. They've forgotten that we are still America, and as soon as we are awake and have returned to common sense, and principle, and the passion for freedom, they're little project is over.

The birth of America was not the birth of a flame that would eventually die out, and it was not the birth of a phase, or an empire. But it was definitely the birth of true hope. Hope cannot come from a single person who promises change, but it does come when a group of people decide that they will stand by faith, freedom, and morality. It was in the hearts of our founders, and I know that along with their passing of this country to generation after generation, they also passed their flame of passion for faith, hope, charity, liberty, honor, integrity, and strength, and I know it is still burning within us today. All we have to do is find it. If we can first, soul-search ourselves, and fix who we are, then we can save this nation. We've already taken the first step in remembering where we've come from. Now let's go even further and remember Who got us there and Who has kept us intact since then.

2

The Cross And The Country

"The time has come to turn to God and reassert our trust in Him for the healing of America. Our country is in need of and ready for a spiritual renewal"
–Ronald Wilson Reagan

The idea that God has shown Himself throughout history has grown more and more controversial over the last few years. Before, it has been quietly disputed, if at all, and was once widely accepted by the American population. But, as we continue to shy away from our morals, we also continue to compromise our foundation as a country which, whether the people in power today like it or not, includes God. We have slowly allowed political correctness, or the idea that what we were built on might "offend someone" to overthrow God's place in our nation. People today get so unnecessarily offended when God's name is evoked in any public building, but why?

You don't hear higher-ups today standing up against the construction of a Ground Zero mosque. No, that would offend people! Instead, you just hear ideas tossed around about taking the phrase, UNDER GOD out of the Pledge of Allegiance.

There's no doubt that the Progressives in power today recognize God's resounding appearance in the history and foundation of our nation, because of how hard they've tried to take Him out of it. To compromise our principles is horrible, but to compromise the rightful place of the One who has single- handedly brought America out of countless hardships and faithfully endured and prospered us as a nation since the day we were founded? That's just scary. God is a part of this nation's history, and our founders were dead set on establishing this country with God as a centerpiece, and His word as our law. Don't listen to my words. Look back on some of the documents from that time period.

John Adams' Massachusetts Constitution of 1780 states, "*As the happiness of a people and the good order and preservation of civil government essentially depend upon piety, religion, and morality, and as these cannot be generally diffused through a community but by the institution of the public worship of God and of the public instructions in piety, religion, and morality.*" That was only Article III, Article II even states, "*It is the right as well as the duty of all men in society, publicly and at stated seasons, to worship the Supreme Being, the great Creator and Preserver of the universe. And no subject shall be hurt, molested, or restrained, in his person, liberty, or estate, for worshipping God in the manner and season most agreeable to the dictates of his own conscience, or for his religious profession or sentiments, provided he doth not disturb the public peace or obstruct others in their religious worship."* Back then, faith was concrete in our nation. That's something that's set in stone. You can't cover it up.

People today can rewrite, revise, and protect us from the truth all they want, but you can NOT change the past. Why keep our nation's founding faith out of the nation? Better yet, when we don't keep it out, and we actually include God in something, why do people treat it as if we've just committed an act of war? There is no constitutional protection from being offended.

There IS a constitutional amendment that protects our freedom to practice whatever belief we may hold, which cannot be superseded. Oh, wait, I'm sorry, my bad. I forgot that one "Separation of Church and State" thing that people keep raving about at the very mention of anything connected to faith that isn't even IN the Constitution. That's right, you won't find it. The Constitution states that, *"Congress shall make no law respecting an establishment of religion, or prohibiting the free exercise thereof."* The term actually originated in a letter written by Thomas Jefferson to the Danbury Baptist Association of Connecticut in 1802, which if you calculate as well as a high school student, was <u>fifteen</u> years after the Constitution was written.

The Danbury Baptists were a minority religion in their state who feared that the state's powers overrode their Constitutional right to practice their beliefs. So, they sought consolation in Thomas Jefferson, who answered back with a letter stating that their religion was as protected as anyone else's, and that *"the constitutional establishment clause created a wall of separation between church and state."* But wait, before progressives start throwing their long-awaited victory party, they should actually read Jefferson's letter. What he meant in that letter, is that religions are protected from the states powers, not the states from religion.

Many of Jefferson's (and other founders') words and lifestyles have been distorted over the last 200 years. Like Jefferson's letter to Dr. Thomas Cooper, which was once shoved in my face, argumentatively, with the quote from said letter: *"Christianity neither is, nor ever was a part of the common law."* Maybe this person engaging me figured I would never take the time to look up the actual text of Jefferson's letter. Jefferson, first of all, was referring to common law throughout world history, not American law. American law was totally separate from the world's law. When America was formed, it was formed as a completely new nation, and system of government. Thomas Jefferson did, himself, live by the Christian faith, so did Thomas Paine whom you'll hear about later on. However, they both lost all credibility in America after their involvement in the French Revolution, because they went about their "faith ideals" the wrong way.

People out there are taking the words of founders out of context in order to make society fit their twisted view of our country. They claim that God has no right to be and was never meant to be a part of this nation, and they are wrong. We are a country based on Christianity and dependent on God. Freedom to express our own beliefs is one of the basest of reasons why we cut ourselves from Britain in the first place, but we as a country, were founded on the principles of the Holy Bible and dedicated to God and the Christian faith. Um, hello? One nation, Under GOD? Singular, as in ONE. Now we have people coming over from other countries and even people already here trying to ram their foreign beliefs down the throats of the American people. Look, I would be the first to stand by them and their right to freely practice their belief, whatever that may be, but what I will never accept is to attempt to take God out of my nation OR my nation's history.

God was there when we came to be. In fact, if not for Him, we never would have come to be in the first place. When we were first coined, we were nothing but thirteen states, and we took down the entire British regime. We brought down a well trained, well financed, and well armed British Militia as nothing but thirteen states. Do you honestly think we did that by ourselves? No, God was there, because our founders relied heavily on the *"protection of divine providence."* Do you know that before anything else, the very first thing that George Washington and the Continental Congress did was to enter into a time of prayer? No, seriously, there's even a painting depicting it, called *"The First Prayer of Congress"* (7) artist unknown. If you would like to look it up yourself, be my guest. In fact, I encourage you to. That goes for everything said in this book; don't take my word for any of it. Do your own research. If you would like to fact-check me to make sure what I say is true, go ahead, PLEASE.

Prayer was the actual beginning to the story of America. Isn't that crazy? Those founding nutcases! Don't they know there's a separation of church and state? What were they thinking? They might have *offended* someone.... oh wait, they DIDN'T CARE. -Our forefathers believed and firmly relied on God to get us through. They understood that God gave us our rights as people, and that without Him nothing could be accomplished.

Unlike the "progressive" (if you'd actually consider it progress) leaders of today, they weren't afraid to hold tightly to God even though what they believed might be offensive to some. Hate to break it to anyone who tries to fight history when it comes to this but, you can't change the past, or the indisputable fact that we were born as an independent nation, dependent on God. In fact, the Founders were so dependent on God, and deep in their trust for Him that the first thing they did was dedicate this nation to Him. *"O Lord our Heavenly Father, high and mighty King of kings, and Lord of lords, who dost from thy throne behold all the dwellers on earth and reignest with power supreme and uncontrolled over all the Kingdoms, Empires and Governments; look down in mercy, we beseech Thee, on these our American States, who have fled to Thee from the rod of the oppressor and thrown themselves on Thy gracious protection, desiring to be henceforth dependent only on Thee.*

"To Thee have they appealed for the righteousness of their cause; to Thee do they now look up for that countenance and support, which Thou alone canst give. Take them, therefore, Heavenly Father, under Thy nurturing care; give them wisdom in council and valor in the field; defeat the malicious designs of our cruel adversaries; convince them of the unrighteousness of their Cause and if they persist in their sanguinary purposes, of own unerring justice, sounding in their hearts, constrain them to drop the weapons of war from their unnerved hands in the day of battle!

"Be Thou present, O God of wisdom, and direct the councils of this honorable assembly; enable them to settle things on the best and surest foundation. That the scene of blood may be speedily closed; that order, harmony and peace may be effectually restored, and truth and justice, religion and piety, prevail and flourish amongst the people. Preserve the health of their bodies and vigor of their minds; shower down on them and the millions they here represent, such temporal blessings as Thou seest expedient for them in this world and crown them with everlasting glory in the world to come. All this we ask in the name and through the merits of Jesus Christ, Thy Son and our Savior. Amen."(5)

This prayer was prayed along with Congress, on

September 7, 1774 at 9:00 am by Reverend Jacob Duche', a chaplain of the Christ Church in Philadelphia, Pennsylvania. What an amazing way to birth a country. The very first thing we are is a dedication to God and God's word, which is our law. It's a part of us, no matter what anyone else would like to believe. God honored this prayer with the birth of freedom, and the birth of a republic. Since then, so much has passed but we have come through scarred, but intact as a country. George Washington, is the first official president of the United States of America. Like anyone with a big name in society or history, a lot has been speculated about him; some bad, some good, some true, and some just flat out ridiculous.

My interpretation of the principled man Washington was, is a man dependent on the ethics of the Christian bible, faith in God, and courage to stand by what he believed in. However, his system of beliefs have been highly disputed and speculated about, because for some reason, people hate the idea that our founders wanted anything to do with religion. Bigotry has officially taken over common sense, and it's sad. All I will say about Washington is what has been proven; that he believed above all things in honor, merit, and yes, God. Washington was the first president of the U.S. and the commander in chief of the Continental Army during the Revolutionary War. Mostly educated through home schooling or tutoring, he received a surveyor's license from William and Mary College in 1748. At age 16, he copied by hand, ***"110 Rules of Civility and Decent Behavior In Company and Conversation,"*** in which, he stated, *"When you speak of God, or His attributes, let it be seriously and with reverence. Honor and obey your natural parents although they be poor."* This is just Washington at an early age.

According to "America's God and Country," by historian William J. Federer, Washington was an active Episcopalian (close to Catholicism). According to records, Washington was in active communion with the Anglican Church, and he served more than twenty years as a trustee, and as church warden on at least three occasions. Being a part of this, he regularly repeated the Apostle's creed, which began, *"I believe in God, the Father Almighty, Maker of Heaven and earth. And in Jesus Christ, His only Son our Lord"* (1). During the revolution, Washington endured all that his men did, but stayed faithful to God the father, whom Washington relied on to get him through these trying times. The American Headquarters on the Hudson River was where Washington prayed this prayer in June of 1779:

"And now, Almighty father, if it is Thy holy will that we shall obtain a place and name among the nations of the earth, grant that we may be enabled to show our gratitude for Thy goodness by our endeavors to fear and obey Thee. Bless us with Thy wisdom in our counsels, success in battle, and let all our victories be tempered with humanity. Endow, also our enemies, with enlightened minds that they become sensible of their injustice, and willing to restore our liberty and peace. Grant the petition of Thy servant, for the sake of Him whom Thou hast called Thy beloved Son; nevertheless, not my will, but Thine be done."

Washington believed in God's power and gave Him the glory for any and all victories achieved. Washington took the oath of office with his hand on a Bible opened to the verse, Deuteronomy 28, which promises blessings for a nation according to its faithfulness to God and His word (2). On April 29, Washington was inaugurated, and after being sworn in, leaned over, and kissed the Bible. It was on October 3, 1789 that Washington issued his first National

Thanksgiving proclamation, his second came on January 1, 1795.

Washington also kept a personal prayer book which consisted of twenty four pages in his field notebook, in which he evokes the name of Jesus Christ multiple times, and refers to Him as God's, *"Beloved Son,"* something for which people are attacked with lawsuits and verbal threats today. On the rear of Washington's tomb is engraved John 11:8, *"I am the resurrection and the life; sayeth the Lord. He that believeth in me, though he were dead, yet he shall live. And whosoever liveth and believeth in me shall never die."* (1)

Another of the founders was Philadelphia's famous radical writer of 1776, Thomas Paine, author of the Pamphlet series entitled, The American Crisis, in which he signed "Common Sense" which actually sparked the entire idea behind our republic. For some reason, because of his passion for the American Revolution, and his rebellion against British tyranny, people today make him out to be one who coined the dangerous progressive movement of today, which was actually started by the communistic Marx brothers. It has been said that he was highly agnostic, and hated any type of religion.

Actually, according to Paine's "Common Sense", Paine was a firm believer in God, and the idea that God's law is the only law that we should be governed by, not the law of any king or tyrant. What Paine actually hated, contrary to popular belief, was not faith in God, but the idea of organized religion or religion being mingled with politics. He believed it crippled one's ability to have an intelligent argument and also ruined the chance for anyone to come to any kind of solution to a problem.

If you look into his writings, like Common Sense, you will find things like, *"The cause of America is in a great measure the cause of all mankind. Where, says some, is the king of America? I'll tell you, friend, He reigns above, and doth not make havoc among mankind like the royal Brute of Britain. Yet that we may not appear defective even in earthly honors, let a day be solemnly set apart for proclaiming the charter; let it be placed on the divine law, the Word of God; let a crown be placed thereon."* Of course, Paine lost all credibility when he published his work, "***The Age of Reason***" which embraced French rationalism. This is another instance in Paine's life and writings, where the speculated idea of his religion- hating atheism comes in. But, if you look in a little further, you'll find that later in his life, he had a bit of a change of heart and wrote, "*I would give words, if I had them, if the Age of Reason had never been published. O Lord, help! Stay with me! It is hell to be left alone*", and eventually dies giving his last words, "*I die in perfect composure and resignation to the will of my creator, God.*"

Understand, that despite all of these facts, and all of this reality, people will still argue to the death that God was not involved in the birth of our nation, nor was He ever meant to be involved in any part of U.S. history. What I don't understand is why it is so hard for some people to comprehend the reality of God's hand and impression in the roots of our country and what I don't understand even more are the people who really just don't want Him there. They don't want to believe any of this despite all He has done for this country. I ask them, what do you have to lose? If you're right, then you're right, you win and it doesn't matter. Everyone goes about their lives. BUT, if you're wrong, and you better hope hard that you aren't, then we as a country are so, SO much better off in His hands, as He's proven since the birth of our nation.

Yes, bad things happen, but only when we turn our

backs on God, will He allow them to go on continually, or without reward in the end. Some of us accept the truth, but we all take God for granted. We put him on the back burner. I'm just as guilty of this. But you have to ask yourself, how long can we go on doing it? Think back to my earlier reference to Washington's swearing in. Deuteronomy 28, as I said, is a promise from God that He will always protect those nations who accept Him and call on Him in times of struggle and look to Him in times of goodness, thanking Him for all He's done. Washington kissed the Bible after being sworn in, as if to be making a solemn vow that this will now and always be a nation founded solely under God. He understood the promise...do we still?

People in power today are doing everything that they can possibly do to keep God out of our Nation. You can go Google that if you really don't believe me. Look up the little tidbit about the 10th Circuit Court of Appeals in Utah, who ruled that the standing of fourteen Christian crosses memorializing the death of highway officers along the side of a highway should be branded unconstitutional as an *"endorsement of religion, implying a state preference for Christianity,"* when the American Atheists sued the state of Utah to have the crosses removed because they *"imply that the troopers who died there were Christians"* (8). Media and higher-ups today are also pushing things like taking the phrase "Under God" out of the American pledge, because well, that's just the past. *"It isn't the 1950's anymore,"* said **Washington Post** columnist David Waters in his article ***"It's Time to Update the Pledge,"*** which attempts to demean the phrase, and America's faith by pinning religion with terrorism and as a dying breed. I think Mr. Waters needs to crack a history book, and do a little research as to WHO America's God is, because I can promise you, He's nothing like the Taliban's "god." God has had His hand on us, as I've said, since the day we were born, and He has a plan for this country, plans to give us hope and a brighter future, and plans to prosper us while all others who don't accept Him fall.

But somewhere along the road from 1776 to today, we've lost sight of our faith. We've allowed it to be challenged without putting up a fight. There are two types of people in American society today: One who accepts the founding faith of America, and one who doesn't. Those who do are in short supply lately and until we find the strength to stand again, our faith is that much closer to being ripped from our homes and nation. Today we look at faith as if it's just something we use every now and then to describe something like a religion, or a person of faith. But what we forget so easily now, is that faith isn't just a describing word or a noun when it comes to the country or to us as individuals. What I mean is, faith is also an action word.

The Bible does not say that we are to sit by faith, or sleep by faith. No, we WALK by faith, putting one foot in front of the other, moving forward in God's plan. No, that doesn't mean moving toward the change of principles and morality, or the way this country was set up to be run. It means that when tough things happen, when we feel down and out, to always look to God, and know that if we allow Him into our lives, He has everything under control. It means to keep believing even when the world around you is telling you to give up.

It's the same for the United States of America as well as for individuals. Bad things have happened but God has brought us through. However, all He has to do is take His hand away, and we're idle; without guidance, and without favor. That is what's going on right now, on your evening news channels, and your bank statements and in your City Halls. We as a country have turned from God, so He has turned from us. Some say if God is so good; if He has such an awesome plan, then why doesn't He just make us listen, why let these bad things happen? Let me ask you...what good is any gift, if it is forced?

God is not a controlling God, He is faithful and just and has the ability to be controlling, but He is not. He will let us make our own decisions if that is what we choose to do. I don't know about the rest of you, but I can't go a day without His guidance, love, or forgiveness. Here's another question, If God is not controlling, what gives us the right to be? Discriminating, demonizing, and violently attacking any other religious groups in the name of God, is wrong, and sick. We aren't going to save people or fix the nation by burning the Quran or any other book sacred to another religion. If someone is doing this, or any other radical act, they should be rejected by the Christian faith. By taking up our cross, is how we find the ability to restore. So let's stop allowing political correctness and the fear of offense to others who may or may not believe what we do, or at least what we were built on, keep us from praising the One who is worthy of it.

I am as guilty as anyone for not giving God the time He deserves, and letting His word be questioned without standing by it. There are Sundays that come when all I want to do is relax in front of the TV. Or when I'm forced to go to church, all I want to do is focus on the hott new girl in the back row, and worry about when service is going to end so I can catch her name and facebook her (yes, ok, I'm still human. Sue me). But, it's wrong. God's time is God's time, and we should take full advantage of it now while we still have the freedom to do so. With the way things are going, the right to practice your beliefs is slowly becoming endangered, and is being swallowed by political correctness and an expanding government. If you need an example of that, just flip on Jon Stewart or MSNBC for a few minutes.

There is no clause in the Constitution that protects someone from being offended, so if they dislike it so much, then I'll be the first to give them a plane ticket to anywhere they would rather go. Because as for ME, in MY country, we will serve the Lord. At the very least, God deserves our gratitude, and time. People have a right to practice whatever they want in this country, and as I said, I would be the first to stand with them protecting that right. But don't take away our country's foundation. NO ONE has ANY right to try and take God out of our history, or out of His place at the head of this nation. Let God back in America, back into our schools, and homes, and political meetings and I promise we will see REAL change occur.

I implore any Christian of any faith, go to your church and pray for America. Pray for us to find God once again, and for the next time we open a book of the past, we not only remember history, but we remember HIS-story. Because of God, this country has not only survived, but we have been renowned throughout history as a promised land to the world. Before we are able to have an economic resuscitation, we are in need of a spiritual one. So, my prayer for America is that we would return to his will, that God would have His way and that we would become once more what made us that symbol of hope, and the shining city on a hill that we once were.

The Washington monument stands erect in Washington D.C., 555 feet tall, as a tribute to Washington's presidency and life. On the peak of the monument, engraved and untouchable, are the words, *"Laus Deo"* which means

"Praise be to God." These words will not fade, and they should never ever be taken from their rightful place, on the arrow of the Washington Monument, pointing to Heaven. They are not visible to the naked eye, and go unnoticed by visitors. Nevertheless, much like God Himself, they are there, watching over America, never to fade away.

3

The Promised Land

"Freedom is the last, best hope of earth."
-Abraham Lincoln

In the new year of 1892, passenger ships loaded to the brim with people from all over the world flocked to a small island near the shoreline of Manhattan. As each ship drew closer to the dock, a tall, erect statue of a crowned woman holding a torch came into view of the passengers. They began to cheer and cry with joy, clutching their families tightly, dreaming about their future at the sight of the statue. They knew that they were in a new place. A place built on freedom, and new opportunity.

They were in America; a place where they could start again, and have a chance to make their dreams come true. This island they were going to is renowned as the most widely populated of the Immigrant stations used by the United States since the first great wave of immigration came to the U.S. in 1815. It is known as Ellis Island and it is estimated that more than 100 million Americans are directly related to immigrants who passed through here during its time as an Immigration station.

However, this chapter isn't about the history of Ellis Island, but more so about the history of the people who came here through it. Immigration wasn't only a dream come true for all of the people coming in, but it is also what helped build our nation into what it has become over hundreds of years; a promised land. The statue that immigrants saw entering into the state of New York in 1892 was, as you probably already guessed, the Statue of Liberty. They became so overwhelmed with emotion at the sight of this statue because to them it was a symbol that they had finally achieved freedom. The statue was a symbol of liberation, and an end to injustice. To them, America was a dream come true compared to where they were originally from. Back then, we were on top of the world. People from all over the world came here, some just for the privilege of being able to say that they lived IN America. Let's compare that viewpoint to how we are viewed today.

Here's a little story for you. I was on Facebook one night. Yeah, believe it or not, I have another life that doesn't involve spending all my time writing all this stuff. Anyway, I was on Facebook reading what someone had written to a half-truthed, left wing news station that I was doing a background check on. He was German, and what he wrote to this program was, "Wow, all the stuff you guys report on over there and stupidity that goes on sure makes me glad that I live in Germany." That struck a deep blow in the pit of my stomach. I couldn't believe someone living 1,466.94 miles away would have such harsh things to say about a country that was once known as a beacon of freedom to all living outside its walls. I commented back, targeting more so, the actual news group and the face-fans of it, than the commentator himself.

I asked them if they were proud of the image they were putting out about us. It shocked and hurt me to see that among all the tea party hating, and FOX news trashing going on, no one had the guts to drop all the political crap for two seconds and stand up for what truly matters: America as a whole. How could they just sit there and allow the verbal abuse of our nation from someone across the globe? The German commentator replied to me, first, with words I won't repeat (yeah, they sure know how to win arguments over in Germany, don't they?), and then trying to tell me that all my "patriotism" was nothing but "anachronistic obliviousness." He said to me that the sooner America has forgotten its embarrassing past, the better off we would be, and he also began to try and explain to me how uneducated, and hopeless we are.

If this display of America's current image to people overseas isn't enough to make people see just how far off we are from where we should be, then I don't know what is. Now, the reason I tell this story isn't to condemn anyone on the left, or accuse them of political bigotry over the good of America, because I'm absolutely certain that some people on the right's side of the court are just as guilty. We all are at one point or another. Even I am at times. The point of telling this story was to illuminate the extreme contrasting of the world wide outlook on America now, and back when people came flooding into what was our safe haven. See, in the 1830's, to the rest of the world, America was a fertile land full of opportunity for individual success.

We were teeming with all sorts of people who came for all different reasons, like voluntary immigrants, who were people that came to us to make a fortune, escape the poverty of their homeland and religious persecution, or find business opportunities unavailable back home. We also were full of young men who came as chain immigrants. They traveled to America to find a job, receive a steady income, and then, once they were settled, send home for the rest of their families to join them. The wave of Immigration to Ellis Island was the biggest to hit the U.S. with people coming from a vast majority of places, like Austria-Hungary, Italy, and Russia. Though this wave ended in 1917, when Congress passed exclusionary laws that aimed to keep out *"undesirable countries or religions."* We then reestablished our immigration policies with some revisions, with the Immigration Act of 1965, allowing all immigrants to enter America as long as they met specific requirements.

The process of Immigration, while strenuous, was worth the work to all of those who took the long journey to get here. They went through draining processes of inspection, in which they were checked to be disease-free, and able to work for a living in their new land. After the health inspection, they were asked about their aspirations and intentions for when they got into the country and if they had any money. They were asked about their past, where they were headed in America, and what their plans were for when they arrived. Once they finished the inspection process, they were able to exchange whatever amount of money they had for American currency. They then were able to gather together their family and whatever luggage they had and begin their new life. But in some sad cases, families were split because of members not passing an inspection. Even so, only about two percent of all immigrants were turned back.

This was when a family was forced to decide to continue on without that member of the family, or turn around with them. This immigration process, while heart breaking at times, was the reason we were known as a "Promised Land." Regardless of race, or religion, everyone got their fair shot at getting to where they wanted to be in life. This was the reason in itself that we are known as a country of hope. In a way, this immigration process sort of defines, the United States. Not only did it help us grow economically, but through allowing people to come, we were able to give people hope, and a brighter future.

We once were the country that stood with open arms to people who needed it most. So what happened? *"I'm excited to go. I want to live in Philadelphia. I want to have a horse. I want to see the Indians. Every thing will be better in America. Lots of food and money for everyone!"* This quote comes from a story I found on a young Italian immigrant's ride over to America on a very big boat. Did you see what she said? Everything will be better in America. Compare that to my previous story, about the German Facebookie. Is the difference between they're vision of this nation as transparent to you as it is to me, or am I just some crazy, oblivious nut? What happened to us? Have we allowed politics and government to take over our humanity that much?

Our current worldwide reputation shows how big-government is destructive to America's vision. We have allowed our focus to centralize too much on pleasing ourselves, and allowed a progressive movement (which I will get into later) to use stimulus and materialism to keep us occupied. We have become like the Roman Empire: Keeping us averted from what's really going on, until inevitable collapse ensues.

People remember the Roman Empire for a lot, including its fall, but what people forget is HOW it fell, and that the destruction of the empire wasn't all that complex. It was actually pretty simple as many political authors have already laid out: People call for more and more government aide, the government expands exponentially, and the economy slows, which makes taxes and prices go up, and currency value drop. The government then begins to weasel its way into civilian home and private life which, as you will learn later, is hardly ever successful. Then people in power begin to divert the public's attention away from inevitable economic destruction with the use of stimulus and materialism. Individual enterprise and willingness to work dies, and finally, BOOM; collapse hits hard. This is exactly what this wild expansion of the U.S. government is driving us toward today. My only prayer is that we are able to veer off of this road soon enough to avoid the same outcome as the Roman Empire.

The only way to do that is to wake up and reaffirm our freedoms in our principles. Despite the failures and setbacks such as the fight over healthcare, the national deficit, or the countless number of pointless stimulus packages, and everything else that we have allowed to go on while we have been asleep, there are still people today who look to America for guidance, and look at us as if we are where Heaven itself lies.

If you are an American doctor and you go to a third world country, the natives look at you already with the idea in their head that you have the ability to miraculously cure anything, just because you ARE an American. We can't let those people down. We need to return to our righteous indignation. Righteous indignation, if you don't already know, is a sort of retributive justice. To me, righteous indignation is anger toward something that I find immoral and wrong. But the key difference between pure anger toward something and righteous indignation is the way we channel our anger: When you choose to try and make a difference with your anger instead of just letting it sit and boil.

Its time to stop sitting and boiling, or sleeping, or just not caring, and its time to bring forth our righteous indignation toward injustice and wake up our charitable hearts and open up our arms to anyone who is in need of a second chance. I think someone should bring back, or at least make a whole new Ellis Island. There are amazing stories from all over this country of people who are standing up for this, and making a difference in lives everywhere. To these people, to anyone who is standing for something they believe in, I applaud you. At the very least, you have earned my respect.

You should know that you and what you do, is a great part of what holds this country to its foundations. We have the ability, and for the time being, the freedom as Americans and as a country to be the "Promised Land" again. The Statue of Liberty, which was the welcoming committee for all Immigrants coming into this country, in one hand holds a tablet, inscribed with the date "JULY 4, 1776" in Roman Numerals, which, if you didn't sleep through the first chapter, you know as the day we celebrate America's independence after officially adopting the Declaration. On the granite pedestal of the statue are the words, *"Give me your tired, your poor, your huddled masses yearning to breathe free. The wretched refuse of your teeming shore. Send these, the homeless, tempest -tossed to me, I lift my lamp beside the golden door!"*

America is the golden door. A land of opportunity to fulfill your dreams. Liberty is a second chance at happiness, and America is the place to have just that. Your chance at what our founding fathers intended for all who enter

America; the chance at Life, Liberty, and the Pursuit of Happiness. We just have to stop hitting the snooze button on our alarm clocks.

4

The American Dream—Then, Now, Always...

"I've always found that anything worth achieving will always have obstacles in the way and you've got to have that drive and determination to overcome those obstacles on route to whatever it is that you want to accomplish."
—Chuck Norris

Walt Disney is renowned worldwide as one of the most influential and successful men of imagination in America. Unless your parents kept you locked in a cellar as a child living on nothing but wood shavings and cheetos, you've at least heard his name. Disney is the great creative mind who brought us all smiles with his famous cartoon characters throughout our childhood and even during the childhood of our own kids. (Not that I would know anything about that yet).

Disney is considered a *"folk hero of the twentieth century."* He represents, in himself and even through his characters, his own ideals such as creativity, imagination, courageousness, and happiness. But, the most important ideal that I believe Walt Disney represents doesn't have anything to do with his happy mouse cartoons or world famous theme parks, attractions, movies, or even his amazing level of creativity, which most artists can only aspire to. The most important thing Disney represents to me is self-made success. Remember the last chapter that was about all of the people who came into America way back when?

I got into a lot of the reasons as to why they all came, and if you remember, a lot of them came chasing their shot at what is called the "American Dream." Now I know that anyone over thirty, who is reading this is probably laughing and thinking, "what could this kid possibly know about self-made success? He's not even out of high school!" Your right about that, I am still trying to survive in high school, and I haven't exactly had the chance to be on my own, in order to know anything about creating success for myself other than what I am able to accomplish under my parent's roof.

Well, let's just say that being blessed enough to grow up by the guidance of men like my pastor, my father, my grandfather - men who have worked hard every day of their lives in order to be where they are now - has given me enormous insight on what the American dream is. Not everything I know about making my dreams a reality have come from my own achievements. A lot of my own personal knowledge comes from observing good, respectful, hardworking people that I know in my own life, and even a few I don't know personally. It's up to you whether or not you wish to accept what I say regarding this subject, but how about making that decision at the end of the chapter?

It is transparently clear to me, even at this age that this American dream is something different for everyone, but the ideal is centered around the same foundations: Self- success, self- sacrifice, and individual struggle. Look at anyone who has ever had REAL success in their lifetime. I don't mean the kind of success that you can buy, or the kind that you're born with or that you can cheat your way to. REAL success is obtained only through ethical decisions, integrity, faith, and a whole lot of self sacrifice. Walt Disney didn't wake up one day and say, "You know, today I think I'm going to create the next world famous cartoon franchise that will eventually take flight as one of the world's most well known character symbols of all time. And maybe I'll coin a couple thousand movies and invent a few world famous theme park attractions while I'm at it."

Not even close. Actually, despite what his first few interviews for cartooning told him, he had artistic talent, no doubt about it. But as anyone with dreams and desires, he began farther away from his goal than Rosie O'Donnell from the salad bar or a library. He first started pursuing a career in art at the McKinley High School in Chicago, putting himself through by selling his premature art to friends and neighbors.

After high school he ended up being rejected by the military because he was under age. So instead, he joined the Red Cross and drove an ambulance for a year in France chauffeuring around Red Cross officials, which was emblazoned in Disney cartoons instead of the usual camouflage. When he returned back home, he pursued a career in commercial art, creating a company called Laugh-O-Grams, which eventually went bankrupt. So, with nothing but a suitcase and twenty bucks, Disney headed to Hollywood for a fresh start, where he was rejected by many before finding success in the cartooning industry. Eventually, he won his FIRST studio Academy Award in 1932, for his production, "Flowers and Trees," which was the first full color cartoon (3).

Even now, after Walt Disney has passed away, looking at the exponentially increasing success of the Disney Empire, Walt Disney had never even imagined his creations would make it as far as they have. But, through self-determination and by proving himself through times of hardship, he achieved his American dream. Today, our youth, and our people are being taught that hard times and struggles are destructive, and that failure shouldn't happen. That's wrong. Failure CAN be destructive, if you choose to see it that way. Failure can also be constructive if you choose to use it. Failure is what gets us where we want to go. I believe that by falling down every once in a while, we learn to pick ourselves up, and learn from our past. The things that happen to us, and the hard times we face don't define who we are, unless we allow them to. What defines us is what we choose to take away from adverse circumstances. Have you ever heard that before Thomas Edison invented the light bulb, he had failed almost one thousand times? When's the last time you heard of someone persevering like that? We don't learn from struggle anymore.

Unless our hopes and dreams are based on principle, dedication, determination, honor, and integrity, they don't mean a thing. I look around sometimes and I'm blown away at our Country's lack of those things. We are in dire need of people with those principles embedded within them. People who are unafraid to stand by integrity and take pride in the way they achieve their dreams. Ever heard of a man named Jon M. Huntsman? If you haven't, you need to. He is the founder of the Huntsman Corporation, a global chemical company, and the inventor of America's first few plastic products, such as the egg carton, the meat tray, and the hamburger clamshell. He is a self-made billionaire, the author of the book "***Winners Never Cheat***," and someone who I believe defines true success.

He appeared on an episode of the Glenn Beck program aired on December 14, 2010, where I learned of the amazing story of a well-known, successful man who, despite trying times, proved that through integrity and honor, one can make a world of difference. Mr. Huntsman grew up in a small house with cardboard walls and outdoor plumbing, but his work ethic was embedded into him in his childhood. His family didn't have much, but his willingness and dedication to hard work was enough to catch the attention of Harold Zellerbach, of Zellerbach Paper Co., who granted Mr. Huntsman a scholarship to the University of Pennsylvania Wharton School of Business, where he learned everything he knows today about the business world. After entering into the business world, before Mr. Huntsman would kick off his chemical company, he had to grow financially. So, he came up with the idea of selling phonograph records over television. Huntsman was the inventor of the first compilation albums, which today would be the CD's of compiled music we see being sold on corny TV infomercials.

He sold millions in the late 1960's and utilized the money to start his chemical company. Somewhere beforehand, he met and married his wife, Karen and had a family. When they were first married, before success fell upon the Huntsman clan, they were very poor, so what little money they had, Karen divvied up, and always sent Huntsman to work with a specific amount of lunch money. He, to my surprise, never failed to take that money and put it, every day, into the mailbox of a neighbor who was worse off than they were. He went without lunch for quite a while but Mr. and Mrs. Huntsman never quit working and never lost faith, or their principles, even when they had nothing. As the success of Huntsman's plastic chemical company began, so did his personal success.

In fact, nowadays, you can find Jon's plastic products in or with items you see every day such as Oreo cookie holding cartons, Ritz cracker wrappers, M&M bags, even Nike sneakers, and those are just a few examples. Actually, you probably can't live a single day of your life without running into one of his products at least once in your daily routine. Mr. Jon Huntsman, however, is not just another business tycoon. Where other successful people go off the beaten path, and step on toes to get ahead, Mr. Huntsman has time and time again, stood firmly by his integrity and his word, and firmly believes in "Business on a Handshake." Huntsman says, *"In life, our word is our bond. Our handshake is the most important ingredient that we have. It's our honor, it's our character, and it's everything about the American dream. If we don't have that, then we don't have life."*

His plan is to die broke, to give all of his money to charity before he passes on. Huntsman has given away $1.2 billion in the last ten years. His largest cause is his cancer institute, which was founded by him and his wife in 1995 in search for a cure. Cancer is a disease that killed his mother, who died in his arms, took the life of his father, stepmother, and has struck him three times, as well. There have been so many rough patches along his road. Mr. Huntsman and his family have been attacked multiple times by hardship. Don't think that life has been a cakewalk for them by any means .

In 1987, tragedy struck the Huntsman family. Jon had given a large amount of money to an institution, which was traced by men who proceeded to scope out his home, while

Jon and Karen were away visiting associates at other plants. Some of their children were there, home from college for Christmas. When 16-year-old, James Huntsman walked out of the house, the men put a pillow case over his head, masking tape around his wrists, and held a knife to his throat as they stole him away from the estate. They then called James' brother, who called emergency services claiming that his brother had been taken and would be viscerally murdered if his father did not pay a million-dollar ransom. Jon was called halfway across the world, and spent all night flying home. When he arrived there, he met with the FBI, who had been stationed all around his home for protection. The rest of the Huntsman children were put into protective custody in different parts of the world. The next morning after Mr. Huntsman returned home, the kidnappers called again, demanding the ransom payment in full.

Huntsman was able to keep them on the line long enough for the FBI to trace the call to a grocery store. When the FBI arrived on the scene, two agents went into the store in an attempt to rescue James. Inside, the kidnapper, who held a knife to James' neck, proceeded to use the knife on one of the agents, burying it deeply into his stomach, nearly cutting him in two. By the end of the struggle, James was safely returned to the family with minor cuts on his neck, and the wounded agent was sent immediately to a hospital. He was forced to retire from the FBI, but received the highest honor the agency had to offer. No money was paid to the kidnapper, but the memory will haunt the family for a lifetime.

Huntsman told this story on the Glenn Beck Program, with tears in his eyes. It was clear that this was something which was extremely difficult for him to speak about. But then, he explained that the first thing he did when his son returned home, was hug him, and call the family together. He explained how they all got down on their knees, cried together, and prayed thanking God for James' safety, and they prayed that the family wouldn't remember this event being connected to charity. This surprised me, because it didn't sound like something a famous billionaire would say on national television.

His words were, "*We weren't going to be detoured in our efforts to make a difference in the lives of others simply because someone had tried to take advantage of us because of a charitable act.*" Jon's incredible story doesn't stop there. The business world hasn't been any easier for him. He has had to save his corporation from bankruptcy several times. In 2008, he faced one of his biggest challenges ever. Jon Huntsman went to bat for his corporation against the Apollo Investment Corporation. The Company had agreed to a buyout headed by Apollo, until Apollo backed out of the deal. This deal would have allowed Jon to fully fund his Cancer Institute, but instead, it made his stock almost worthless. Thankfully, he won in court, and was able to fund his Cancer institute. However, because of Huntsman's dealings with rough patches such as these, he has come to the realization of some of the biggest problems with America's business world.

"*Today, I believe that the financial capitalist of the world's problem is that their goal is accumulating money for the sake of accumulating money, and not for the sake of utilizing it to help their fellow men and women. If your goal is beyond making money, its fun, and really enjoyable. You work twice as hard, your enthused, and your excited, but if it's for the sake of accumulation of money, for one reason or another, you lose the spirit.*" Despite all the struggles and hardships Mr. Huntsman has faced, to this day he continues to stand by his principles and holds tightly to his integrity. Jon also says, "*There is just an ethical aspect about life that if we're straight with each other, then we're straight with our God, and we're straight with our families.*"

For this chapter, I could have droned on and on about ethics in the real world as well as the business world, and how important I think they are, but you already get that I think they are important. What matters is that YOU SEE how important they are and realize that they are the very best suited guidelines for the restoration of the nation.

I chose Jon M. Huntsman - a capitalist and honorable philanthropist, but also a principled man of God, with an incredible sense of charity and integrity - as an example because I believe that he, and people like him are what the American dream embodies. I chose him because he is a major well-known success story that people can learn from. But he certainly isn't the only story out there. I know people, amazing people in my family, and my mentors and friends, that live every day life through the best in themselves. Despite how hard things get around them, they remain hinged to their principles. And its people like that who keep this country afloat. One ideal that President Obama's administration has had is true; that through economic hardship, we all have to band together and help each other out.

However, their idea of that is stealing money from people who have earned it, and splitting it between the rest of the population. That's not charity, that's stealing, and it's wrong. That's not only stealing from people who have earned what they have, but that's also setting those who receive this aid up for failure, because when people become dependent on government aid, they lose the ability to work for themselves. They lose their ethic, their pride and livelihood, and eventually when the money runs out, everything else they own.

The job of the government isn't to prevent failure, it's to aid us only when we truly need it. It isn't about taking people's earnings and spreading them out to everyone else. That's thievery. It's about earning your own life through a hard day's work every day until you make your American dream come true. It isn't about achieving success, never ever slipping up, and becoming rich, and it isn't about when you get there. It's about how you get there, and how you come out in the end. Doesn't that just sound like common sense? Things are tough, and they hurt, but what we need to realize is that the bad things in our life are nothing but a chain reaction that is completely up to us. Meaning that if we look at it, we see that things happen the way they do, and that they are the chain that brings us to who we become as people.

It works by realizing that If this one hard thing I faced in my life hadn't happened, then it wouldn't have led to this part of my life, and so on and so forth, and I wouldn't be where I am today. This chain can go either way as far as the ultimate end result; it's all about the decisions you make. It's whether or not you choose to make the right choices and make a difference in your life instead of just going wherever the road takes you. Are you going to take an easy road for a few years of the good life now? Or, like a real success story, will you sacrifice, and do what you need to do, and choose to stand for honor and, by ethics, to inherit a life even more amazing later on. And maybe, even leave a legacy for youth like me?

Because of what I've been blessed to have been taught at an early age, I choose to learn from my mistakes, and to remember my history. Given, I mess up from time to time, but I always find my path again. That is what we need to allow our mistakes to teach us. We don't need our government to try to keep us from making mistakes, we need our mistakes to help us find our way back onto the right path. We need to stop preaching against individual struggle, because it is through individual struggle that we gain individual success, and in some cases, even united success.

This may sound like a corny cashmaster's infomercial, but DON'T let hard times drag you down. Choose to take away from the toughness, instead of letting it take away from you. No matter what happens, don't close off your heart because of something going wrong in life. Even if it seems like everything that could go wrong is, and everyone and their sister-in-law is against you, hold tight to your word and your heart, and never let a selfish act from someone else close off your heart or your morality.

What people today have forgotten is that the answers to all of our problems have already been answered. They have been written for us in our past. America's founders knew just where to hide all the answers to future problems: In plain sight of those willing to look. The answers have been rooted in our documents, our laws, our history, our music, and our faith. Radio and television host Glenn Beck, said it best when he referenced the third verse of "America the Beautiful":

"Oh beautiful for heroes prove
In liberating strife
Who more than self their country loved
And mercy more than life
America, America may God thy gold refine
Till all success be nobleness
And every gain divine"

Heroes don't become heroes by being born that way. They become heroes by proving themselves through times of struggle and times of greatness. They become heroes by believing not only in themselves, but in something much more than themselves. Something like the change that can be made if just one person chooses to stand up and bring together the passion of humanity and humility in everyone else. Today, our honor and belief in this concept is suffering. We are at a pivotal moment in which a choice must be made. We need to raise more men like Jon Huntsman. We need to raise more George Washingtons, Ben Franklins, and Walt Disneys. We need to return to our noble successes. The American dream is not a house on a hill with a sidewalk of gold. It is a story, an embodiment, of how one person, one country, can be the hope that someone else needs.

5

A United Homefront Against Terror

"We must indeed hang together, or most assuredly we will all hang separately"
–Benjamin Franklin

Terrorism is a subject today in which, just the mention of the word, could spark passionate discussions on all sorts of different ends of the spectrum. Its extreme delicacy as a subject of debate is something that brings out either one's emotional patriotism, hatred, fear, or bigotry. What I mean is that it has a different effect on everyone. The only problem with that is how much it divides us. In the past, America has faced enormous tragedy and adversity ignited by terrorizing acts from radicals, and extremists both foreign and domestic. However, what makes America strong is its unbreakable spirit that remains unafraid of looking evil in the eye, and taking it down.

I've seen it in my own lifetime. When the infamous acts of 9/11 occurred; it struck a major blow to the Republic and its people, as I'm sure we all agree. But do you recall what happened after that day? Through tears of pain in losing nearly three thousand innocent lives on that horrific day in the sick and twisted events that took place, people still found the courage to stand up against these acts of terror.

Nineteen insane men driven solely by evil and cowardice thought they could break us down. These men wanted nothing more than for their acts to be our downfall and to tear us apart from the inside out. But, though our hearts were broken, our spirits remained strong and we allowed our strength to unify us as our American pride took wave over the country in place of our brokenness. Famous Musicians began releasing more patriotic singles, churches started packing out on Sundays, candle light vigils and prayer meetings were being held across the country. We started seeing more flags around public places and homes, more patriotic bumper stickers became relevant and new slogans incited, such as, "these colors don't run" and "Never enough dust to cloud our freedom." A brutal act of terror that could have destroyed us instead brought us closer together. People began rallying up in support of the war on terror against the monsters that were responsible for taking a blow at OUR country.

We began to make it transparently clear to them, and anyone across the globe that the United States is the WRONG cage to rattle. If you mess with us, we will come back with full force, because no person, battalion, group, or regime in the world can shake the American strength and pride. People began pitching in with the brave firefighters and law enforcement officers already taking part in the cleanup in New York City, and memorials honoring the heroic victims lost in the disaster began going up. September 11, 2001 will forever be remembered as a day of disaster, but the people that fought through the pain and punches will forever be remembered as heroes, and regardless of all the hurt and destruction that the terrorist group Al Qaeda brought into OUR homeland, what I will take away the most from September 11, and what I hope all Americans would, is the great courage and unity we showed in the months following, and how the iconic Twin Towers, taken from us that day, will always be remembered for the hope and happiness they brought us, instead of how they were taken.

During the period of the Cold War, The free Capitalist system of the United States was being threatened by a large outburst of communism in Moscow and Beijing, which led to the consideration of a world trade facility to center America's economic system. In 1966, construction of the World Trade Center began. The Twin Towers themselves were designed by Minoru Yamasaki, a Japanese American who was born into a rough life in Seattle in 1912. He was another example of the American Dream. When he was old enough to work, he worked in a Salmon cannery for seventeen cents an hour to put himself through school at the University of Washington, until he found the answer to his prayers. The project itself was completed in 1973, but in the beginning of their life, the towers weren't exactly "New iPhone" popular, they were more like "Polka music" popular. Only a very small select few were in favor of them, others thought they were either too astringent in appearance, or gave little scope for enjoyment, and of course, since it IS New York City, soap-in-mouth worthy words were used about them.

All the critics, however, were eventually won over by the Towers' notability, unlike polka music. Famous icons made frequent visits and entertained in the night clubs on the high, like John Lennon, Frank Sinatra, Liza Minnelli, and Mick Jagger. Stunts were also performed on the towers. Its most renowned is that of a French aerialist named Philippe Petit, who walked a tight rope stretched across at 1,350 ft. between the two towers in 1974. The World Trade Center slowly and surely began to take on the role of a national symbol, and like most national symbols, became the potential target of terrorism. Unfortunately, through deep tragedy, these two iconic symbols of America were taken from us by madmen involved with the Muslim terrorist group al-Qaeda led by the, thankfully late, Osama Bin Laden.

At 5:45 AM, on September 11, 2001, Mohamed Atta, and Abdulaziz Alamari, boarded a plane to Boston in an airport in Portland ME, and by 8:47 AM, American Flight 11, pumped to the brim with 20,000 gallons of jet fuel rammed into the first tower of the World Trade Center, killing 92 people aboard and destroying ten floors of the building. At 9:02 am, the South Tower is hit and everyone realizes that anything that had taken place up to that point had been no accident. At 9:41 AM, flight 77 hits the Pentagon in Arlington, VA, and nine minutes after that, the South Tower collapses. At 10:28 am, the North Tower is taken as well. How these men made it as far as they did is unclear to me and I will make no speculation regarding it because that is not what's important about the date of September 11, 2001.

Construction of a memorial is still in an ongoing process today. The plan for this memorial consists of two of the largest man made waterfalls in the U.S. running down the inside of the footprints of the Twin Towers. Inside, will be the names of the lost that day in the World Trade Center, the Pentagon, and those lost on February 26 in the 1993 World Trade Center bombing. The pools are each nearly a full acre, and also will have parapets of names surrounding them for family, and friends, and co-workers' names to be inscribed next to one another. A Memorial Plaza filled with nearly 400 trees, whose leaves will change from green to blood red in September, will surround the memorial site and separate it from the sounds of the city outside.

Next to the memorial site, my favorite part is being built: A skyscraper to be called the "Freedom Tower." The plan is for it to be constructed taller than either of the Twin Towers. It will stand 1,776 ft, 102 stories, and is estimated to be completed by the year 2013. It will stand as a beacon in New York City, for citizens and newcomers alike, and will represent that no matter how hard you knock us down, we WILL dust off, and we will stand up taller and stronger than we were before. That's what a real united home front is, what we need to be in the face of adversity; people who stand up against it and aren't afraid to fight against injustice against their homeland and look back on the losses, not allowing their sacrifices to be in vain.

But today, everyone is too preoccupied with the politics of terrorism, the controversy of events of it, and the fabricated conspiracy theories of who had their hand in the cookie jar. On September 11, four passenger jets took flight within forty two minutes of one another. Nineteen Islamic Extremists managed to hijack and use these planes as weapons of war to deliver a vile blow to the American public. Two planes took with them two national icons, another was driven into the U.S. Pentagon building, and one was aimed for the White House - but because of the brave, heroic indescribable courage of the passengers on Flight 93, it was taken down in a field outside Pittsburgh. All four planes had one common target, however, which they all succeeded in viscously taking from us; our friends, family members, neighbors, and heroes.

My heart goes out to all to whom this applies, and you have my earnest prayer of peace and my biggest respect for anyone you lost on that day. I know that no matter how many times you hear this, it will never fill the void, but just take me at my word. You are another layer of our country's still standing foundation, because unlike the rest of us, you refuse to remember that day as a possible conspiracy, a political stunt, or a thick, new file of statistics. You look back on that day as a day of mourning and remembrance, and every day after; a day of strength and American pride.

As for the rest of us at this point, September 11, is long forgotten. When it comes to days of infamy like this, we forget, we brush it off because it's the past. Either that or we only look at it from the political perspective or an outlook of hate. We fight the truth of the issue, and split hairs when it comes to speaking about it. We allow it to eat away at us until we either hate anyone of the same descent as the executioners of the attack, we fear being in the same room with one, or we have completely handed over our society to them. The men who committed those acts of terror were vile and wicked, and should be shamed rather than considered a part of any religion or group other than that of a terrorist.

The problem with Americans today is that we either largely discriminate against Muslims, or give them a great amount of rope to walk on us. Given, there are very good Muslim people in America who ask for nothing more than their fair chance at happiness in this country, which they deserve just like everyone else. Unfortunately, there are also those Muslims who do nothing but pull the race/religion card every time they don't get their way or someone brings up the attack of the World Trade Center.

I will tell you this much, Muslim people deserve a fair shot here and their right to practice their religion, as long as it doesn't impede on our rights as Americans. What we as a people should not do is discriminate, OR allow them to walk on the flag. I'll put it this way: You're a die-hard major league baseball fan, someone who follows the sport religiously. You have all sorts of different merchandise decorating the walls at your home, and maybe a car bumper sticker or six. But, a lot of your friends are die-hard fans of the National Football League. So, does that mean that, when you host a house party, you take down all of your baseball posters and pennants, and hide all of your baseball jerseys so you don't offend them? Or, maybe take another route and cut them out of your life and keep them away from your family because they believe Tim Tebow could take Matt Holliday?

No, because both of those ideas lack morality and common sense. Besides, everyone knows Holliday could take Tebow with one arm tied behind his back. Regardless, the same principle applies for the country. We have no right to discriminate against people for their beliefs because it's a right we all have in this country, granted to us by God. However, for someone to build a mosque, a church of the Muslim religion, on the sacred grounds of the Towers' resting place is nothing more than a slap in the face to the nation. A lot of people aren't aware of this fact, but did you know, many places that Muslim people build a Mosque is where they believe they've had a victory in war? That would be like building a Japanese aircraft manufacturer near Pearl Harbor, or tee-peeing a rival high school and placing your high school's mascot on the top. What would the Japanese say if we decided to build a WWII tribute to American soldiers on the ruins of Nagasaki? You think they would just let that happen?

No, that's wrong, and we wouldn't do that because we understand that it's wrong, so why are we allowing people to do it to us? Through the fear of offending someone, we have booted out our good friend common sense on many more issues besides this one, which I will get into later. We have to find a middle ground somewhere between these. One where we aren't afraid to stand up against political correctness, an enormous lack of respect, and an even bigger lack of common sense, but we still don't trample on the freedoms they have.

We need to wake up and remember that while there are many decent Muslims in America, there are also those who seek to decentralize and reform it, as well as the rest of the world, to Sharia. Sharia is the Islamic law. Under this law, adulterers are stoned, men have the right to hit women, women are not allowed to leave the house without a male escort for safety (even though if they are caught without one, they are killed by government officials), and anyone who says anything against the Islamic belief, is to be killed immediately. There is no freedom of religion or speech. It's either Islam, or death. There is nothing "American" about this law, and it plays as an enemy to the democratic way of government. This law seeks to destroy any nation or person who disagrees with this set of beliefs. This law is violent, dictatorial, and still somehow is being pushed and spread out across the globe, and uprooted in our homeland.

Make no mistake, the ways and tactics that these people use to spread this practice, "Jihad", involves blood, and massive loss of life if necessary. They believe that their uses of violent tactics, including explosions, decapitations, or even the use of "children bombs" as they call them, are justified means of spreading their practice of Sharia. Research shows that in June of 2010, the number of child insurgents in Afghanistan had increased five-fold. Kids are being used by Islamic extremists by the age of five.

According to an article in "*The Telegraph,*" a world news source, two kids under ten years of age were spotted in the middle east by surveillance cameras while placing an IED, or improvised explosion device, in a hole and covering it up with dirt.

Of course, if you ask news writer, Barry Dennis of ***Socyberty***, the cleric "Children bombs" could very well mean a Muslim "population explosion." After all, as we all know, SO many Muslim terms have hidden meanings. Yeah, right. I'm not calling out Mr. Dennis for questioning. Our questions are one of our most crucial tools in today's society. The problem arises when we allow those questions and opinions, which Dennis openly states; his faith in this "hidden meaning," to blind us to fact and the real truth. We cannot blind ourselves to the fact that there is an enemy we face out there. Sharia is based on the religious Muslim book, the Quran. The Quran is said to hold over 109 verses that suggest the graphic murder, and violent discrimination of all of us "infidels." I only wish I could include them all, but I don't feel like paying the publisher any extra money. So here are just a few of them. See if you can see what I do:

- *"Soon shall We cast terror into the hearts of the Unbelievers, for that they joined companions with Allah, for which He had sent no authority." Quran 3:151*

- *"Fight them, Allah will punish them by your hands and bring them to disgrace..." Quran 9:14*

- *"They but wish that ye should reject Faith, as they do, and thus be on the same footing (as they): But take not friends from their ranks until they flee in the way of Allah (From what is forbidden). But if they turn renegades, seize them and slay them wherever ye find them; and (in any case) take no friends or helpers from their ranks." Quran 4:89*

- *"The punishment of those who wage war against Allah and His messenger and strive to make mischief in the land is only this, that they should be murdered or crucified or their hands and their feet should be cut off on opposite sides or they should be imprisoned; this shall be as a disgrace for them in this world, and in the hereafter they shall have a grievous chastisement." Quran 5:33*

- *"I will cast terror into the hearts of those who disbelieve. Therefore strike off their heads and strike off every fingertip of them." Quran 8:12*

- *"And the Jews say: Ezra is the son of Allah; and the Christians say: The Messiah is the son of Allah; these are the words of their mouths; they imitate the saying of those who disbelieved before; may Allah destroy them; how they are turned away!" Quran 9:30*

- *"O you who believe! Fight those of the unbelievers who are near to you and let them find in you hardness." Quran 9:23*

I think you get the point. These are nothing like what I've read in my Bible. Muslims are not only taught to brutally murder and violently reject those who disbelieve in their faith, but they are pressed to enforce and spread Sharia to the world using any form of Jihad they can, which unfortunately for us, comes in many more forms than just the use of suicide explosions. Sharia is being spread and weaseled into our courts and our media. So how exactly does this Islamic law weed itself into our nation, a nation of freedom, love, and faith, when Sharia is and has been known as a public enemy to America's system? Well, today there are groups who are passing themselves off as "moderate" Muslim groups, who claim to strive to find only peace, brotherhood, and middle-ground between America and Islam, when their true objective is to spread the practice of Sharia into the American system.

Groups such as the Muslim Brotherhood are openly accepted by today's administration, simply because they come with a "moderate" label. However, as the Bible says, you can only serve one God. You can only believe in one set of ethics, you can't contradict law. As long as you are standing by and pushing the law of Sharia, you cannot stand by anything peaceful, or prosperous. But America today has been so blind-spotted by the idea of inclusiveness that we have shot ourselves in the foot. We now, as Americans, own the number one transmitter of Sharia-compliant banking, and we bought the company as tax-payers: AIG. AIG was taken over by the Government in 2008, and is the largest source of Sharia-compliant banking in America. In other words, we as taxpayers are funding terrorism and Jihad. America has become one of the top Sharia-compliant banking nations in the world. Sharia-compliant banks in America include, of course AIG, as well as Deutsche Bank AG, Dow Jones & Company, Goldman Sachs, INVESCO Perpetual, Julius Baer group, Merrill Lynch & Co., and many, many more are on the list. The length of this list would scare the crap out of any awake American, and the amount of Jihadists funding corporations in OUR own nation is staggering. We, as Americans, have become too comfortable with this idea of "inclusiveness," that in the end, we won't be the ones who were known to be inclusive; we'll be the ones who screwed ourselves over by blinding ourselves to the open threat of Sharia infiltration. There is a way to keep from demeaning and excluding the good Muslims, while standing up to the ones who desire our downfall. We just have to reconnect as a people, and unify.

Don't get me wrong, multiple faiths are being deteriorated by radicals across the U.S. and the rest of the world. It doesn't matter as to what you label yourself. If you are justifying the death of innocent people with religion, you are rightfully pinned as a terrorist. People like that are not Christians, or Muslims, or Buddhists. They are religious zealots, and they should be rejected by everyone. I ask the good Muslims of America to stand up against the inhumane who are embarrassing your faith. If there was a person out there killing people and labeling themselves as Christian, like the murderer of Abortionist George Tiller, I would be the first to boldly and publicly denounce and reject them as nothing but a violent terrorist, though I wildly disagree with abortion.

The solution to our division lies in boldness to stand by our pride, morality, remembrance, and the truth. We cannot be afraid to teach the history of 9/11 and terrorism in schools; and when we do, we must leave out the racial bigotry, and the political correctness. Do it with nothing in your heart besides truth and honor for the day, rather than hatred for the religion. If they are "offended," that's all on them. All you are doing is speaking truth. Don't speculate, but fact-check, research, and then use THAT as your weapon, rather than violence or hatred.

Another issue: Don't ever tell half of the truth. When I was taught about the history of the Attack on Pearl Harbor, I got the short end of the educational stick because instead of being taught that the consequences of the Japanese attacks on December 8, 1941, left America bleeding with the loss of 2,403 American militants, 188 lost planes, and a crippled military fleet of 8 battleships either damaged or destroyed,

I was taken right to the bombing of Hiroshima, and how "unjust and wicked" America was in taking that action. In doing my own research and back-checking all sources, I found the real truth.

Before August 6, 1945, which is the day a 9,700 lb. uranium bomb named "Little Boy" was detonated 1,900 ft. above the city of Hiroshima, thousands of leaflets (little slips of paper with notes) were dropped over Nagasaki and Hiroshima, warning its citizens to evacuate. The U.S. warned them that if they did not evacuate, they would suffer a soon impending doom. The reason we dropped the Atomic bombs was not only to retaliate for our losses in the bombing of Pearl Harbor, but even more to save millions of lives, both American and Japanese. If you research the fighting style of the Japanese military of WWII, they were more than ready and willing to fight to the bitter end, no matter how vicious they had to make it, or how immoral things had to become for anyone caught in the crossfire. In that end, a lot of people would have lost their lives.

That's why I hate half truths, because they put ideas in the minds of MY generation that aren't supported by an ounce of fact, and are only fabrications of people who don't back up what they say but instead live their lives worrying about whom they may offend next. That is what is dividing us. In school today, when September 11 rolls around, my heart is heavy. Most teachers refuse to talk about it because of its "controversy." All we have all day is a few moments of silence over the intercom. I appreciate and respect that, but in my mind, and I'm sure in the hearts of people who lost someone that day, 9/11 deserves a lot more than a few moments of silence. When History becomes something that is controversial, that is a lit-up road sign that our society is suffering, and our principles are slipping.

American people need to stop arguing over the controversy and politics of these days and start seeing them as they deserve to be seen; dark days that we as a country came through together. To take a day of tragedy, to take any tragedy at all and "play politics" with it is disrespectful and pathetic for all of us, and it needs to stop. We need to find and reaffirm our grasp on sanity. True, we have been scathed and hurt by terrorism, and madmen, but through presenting a united front, we have pulled through together when we most needed to. Today I fear that we have lost the ability to do that, have fallen into the pit of division, and we won't be able to pull ourselves out until we accept our old friend common sense again. As I've said before, some people around the world still look up to us.

So, let's forget political correctness and start teaching history through truth because until we start doing that again, we will be divided. Without truth, we have nothing, and the people in power today are keeping it from us. What we need to remember is that in the past, America hasn't come through because of bailouts, stimulus packages, or the constant freebies that are being given to us today by people in power to try to keep us asleep.

We have come through because of God, and because of people who stood by integrity, and who weren't afraid of telling the intangible truth, regardless of how some may view it, for the good of the country. And it is through knowing the truth that we have been able to come through as one united nation. One of the most crucial parts of rescuing America is truth, and through truth, we find something even more important - unity. In the song "***Have you Forgotten***," by Darryl Worley, there are the words, "*Some say this country's just out looking for a fight. Well after 9/11 man, I'd have to say, that's right.*" Don't forget that each and every day, we fight for our honor, and integrity, as well as the freedom that we claim to hold so dearly. We cannot allow the sacrifices of those before us to be in vain. The next time you hear about a day such as 9/11 brought up in a conversation, think back to where you were that day, and how you found out. Then, take time to remember the brave people that we lost that day, and speak of it as it should be spoken of: A day to remember, and a time not forgotten.

6

A Fine Line

"Once we know that people are human, and have some 'Homer Simpson' in them, then there's a lot that can be done to manipulate them."
-Progressive Regulatory Czar,
Cass Sunstein, Aug. 26, 2010

Picture this: It's the bottom of the ninth inning at a home game at Busch Stadium. The grass is freshly cut, the sun is out, fans are on the edge of their seats and a home game between the St. Louis Cardinals and the Chicago Cubs has come down to the wire. The game is tied and the Cardinals are at bat. The Dominican Dream, Albert Pujols, steps up to the plate against Cubs' pitcher Ryan Dempster. Then all of a sudden, Cardinals' team manager Tony LaRussa halts the game. He goes to the plate to tell Pujols that he's decided he doesn't want to give him the burden of the chance to strike out and lose.

Instead, he takes the bat from Pujols, has him go sit on the bench and raises the bat ready to swing at the next pitch in Pujols' place. Sound crazy? Yeah, you'd think so wouldn't you? But, that is exactly the way that the American people are being viewed right now by people higher up. They've decided that we aren't smart enough to think for ourselves, and that if we are given the chance to do so, we'll fail, and ruin everything. So, instead, they come in to do our thinking for us. They tell us to just sit back, they'll do all the big, scary grown up stuff that we just can't handle, because somehow, they're all so much smarter than we are.

See, just like Albert Pujols who has a natural, if not incredible, ability when it comes to the game of baseball, the founders of America stood by the proven fact that people are born with the ability to govern and think for themselves. They believed that the American people are smart enough to know the difference between right and wrong, yes and no, and sensibility and stupidity. Yeah, ok, I agree. Lately it feels like that last one's a bit of a stretch. But, our patriot patriarchs stood firmly by the belief that it was NOT government's job to do the thinking for them, regardless of how ignorant some people really are in today's society, which is another reason we cut ourselves from the tyranny of Great Britain. Government, much like the job of a baseball coach, is not to play the game for us. Government's job is to help align the rules for us, and support us only when we truly need it. Doesn't that just sound like common sense?

Yeah, AGAIN, you'd think so. But today, we are allowing a power hungry group, who believe that people have no control over themselves, their decisions, or they're desires, to step in and play the game for us. The game that we all have been born with the ability to play: Self education.

These people don't only oppose the Constitution. No, if

you oppose the Constitution, that makes you American. See the founders had high expectations for the U.S. They knew that inevitably we would grow and become bigger. But, with social and economic growth, also comes new issues. Issues they knew eventually the Constitution could not cover. Which is why, when the Constitution was written, the founders set up a process in which the people had the option of revising certain parts if necessary. You oppose, and then you change, according to the way the Constitution is set up: The Amendment Process. These people not only oppose the Constitution, they see it as a barrier, or an obstacle. They want to set up, as they've called it, a "New World Order," one that only they benefit from.

One of the biggest threats and enemies to America today is Progressivism. This group I'm referring to are progressives, and they are the ones who are running the reconstruction of our nation while we are sleeping. In fact, they are the ones in charge of putting us to sleep in the first place.

First, let's start with when this disease entered the country. Progressivism first publicly and powerfully showed itself in America when a man named Woodrow Wilson was elected into the position of president of the United States. While he is not the father of progressivism, he IS the one who strengthened it exponentially through his presidency. Woodrow Wilson to me, is one of the most dangerous presidents we have ever seen as a country. At the time, his newfound idea of "progress" set the course for a party whose ultimate goal is to change, basically destroy, the foundation on which America was built. How could one person change America from a country based on the idea of faith, ethics and morality, into a nation dependent on stimulus and materialistic things? Well he didn't do it alone, but he definitely sparked the movement toward so-called "progress."

Wilson is infamous for a lot of things. According to Civil War historians, Wilson was known for endorsing racism, and the movement of the infamous Ku Klux Klan. I am simply stating the facts. In fact, Wilson's two-volume book, published in 1802, entitled "***A History of the American People***," shows off his racism. It states, in Wilson's own words, "*The white men were roused by a mere instinct of self preservation ... until at last there had sprung into existence. A great Ku Klux Klan, a veritable empire of the South, to protect the Southern country.*" According to a few historians, Wilson once had a private screening of the pro-Ku Klux Klan film, "***Birth of a Nation***" in the White House. In fact, the film was a silent movie, and many of the intertitles of the film were drawn from Wilson's "***History of the American People***." The KKK's popularity soared during Wilson's term, and blacks began not only getting the short straw in society, but became major victims of violence as well. During his term, Wilson fired fifteen black people in federal job positions, and replaced them with white people. Besides his racism, Wilson was largely known for having a disturbing superiority complex. He was a narcissistic elitist who convinced himself that he was better, and smarter than others.

He once told William McCombs, Democratic Committee head at the time, "*God ordained that I should be the next president of the United States. Neither you, nor any other mortal or mortals could've prevented this.*" (4) Wilson glorified himself, and craved for power. As he so eloquently put in his book, "***Congressional Government: A Study of American Politics***," '*I cannot imagine power as a thing negative and not positive.*' Hmmm ... nope, no matter how eloquently you put it, it's still pretty crazy to say out loud. And pretty scary if the leader of your country is the one saying it. Power never a negative thing? Do I even have to give a reason why that's crazy? Much like the progressives of today, Woodrow Wilson didn't see people as people. He saw them as pawns that are easy to manipulate.

If you give them enough of what controls them, you can control their emotions, desires, even their futures. He did not believe that individuals had rights ordained by God, nor did he believe they deserved them. He once wrote, *"No doubt, a lot of nonsense has been talked about the inalienable rights of the individual, and a great deal that was mere vague sentiment and pleasing speculation has been put forward as fundamental principle."* (6) Wilson didn't believe that freedom was the solution for anything. He believed instead, that the government was the answer to all of our nation's problems and was oblivious to the fact that it actually was BECOMING the problem. He spread progressivism throughout all sorts of different areas in the nation: Economic, education, social gatherings, his speeches and public addresses, etc. Another thing he sparked was the Progressive movement's hatred for the U.S. Constitution because the Constitution stopped specific aspects to Wilson's fundamental changes, which the American public would have found ... well lets just say not too "Constitutional."

"Living Political Constitutions must be Darwinian in structure and in practice. Society is a living organism and must obey the laws of life. It must develop. All that PROGRESSIVES ask or desire is permission, in an era when 'development' or 'evolution' is the scientific word, to interpret the U.S. Constitution according to the Darwinian Principle." You can pick and choose fancy words as much as you want, but if this is what's coming out of your mouth, you may as

well just tell the truth flat out. We're not stupid, we know what it means.

Thank you Mr. Wilson, this is a perfect example of the progressive movement's antagonistic view of the Constitution. They aren't suggesting the use of the amendment process. What Wilson is asking for is control of the reconstructing of a document that shaped who we are. It doesn't matter what words you use: "Evolving," "Developing," or whatever. Changing is changing, and if you aren't doing it the way it was set up for us, then you are an enemy to the Constitution.

During a campaign speech in 1912 in Scranton, Pennsylvania, Wilson said this, *"Of course this was intended to be a government of free citizens and of equal opportunity, but how are we going to make it such? That is the question. Because I realize that while we are followers of Jefferson, there is one principle of Jefferson's which no longer can obtain in the practical politics of America. You know that it was Jefferson who said that the best government is that which does as little governing as possible, which exercises its power as little as possible. And that was said in a day when the opportunities of America were so obvious to every man, when every individual was so free to use his powers without let or hindrance, that all that was necessary was that the government should withhold its hand and see to it that every man got an opportunity to act as he would. But that time is passed. America is not now and cannot in the future be a place for unrestricted individual enterprise."*

I don't think he could be any clearer if he had a bullhorn. This is how progressives view the principles of self governing and individual success that our founding fathers believed in. Progressives believe that individual enterprise is actually an obstacle, and should be restricted, rather than something that makes an economy grow.

Not only did Wilson's own words prove his hatred for the American system, but his actions did as well. During his reign, he took every part of humanity in America, and made some "government revisions." His control was so out of hand that he created "new standards of manhood" meaning that he would try to regulate what was the right way for people to speak, work, live, and even eat. (Wait a second, who does that remind me of? Certainly not the current administration).

Make no mistake. While the massive $27 billion debt that Wilson left behind was eventually reduced by following presidents, he also left behind a seed of progressivism which has sprouted into one of the biggest threats America faces today. There were more who held some of Wilson's progressive ideals beforehand, such as Theodore Roosevelt, who was known for relocating the 25th infantry regiment of black veterans to a town in Texas in the infamous "Brownsville Incident" of 1906.

The people of Brownsville weren't too thrilled about the relocation, which resulted one night, in a small riot which led to a death and several injuries. Twelve soldiers of the 25th regiment were imprisoned. After the riot, the soldiers who participated were asked to come forward or speak up about those involved. None complied, and no one spoke. The entire regiment was charged with insubordination, and the entire regiment was discharged dishonorably. However, since he needed a fair amount of the black population's approval, Roosevelt did not act on the outrage of blacks across the country until after the congressional election ended. He then officially signed all 167 soldiers dishonorably discharged, their pensions cancelled, and any owed back pay denied, even though the evidence showed that several hours before the riot had even occurred, a commanding officer had reported all soldiers in their bunks and accounted for.

Real stand up guy, huh? Now that you know the beginning of progressivism in the U.S., you need to understand the mindset of the movement. As I've said, knowing the enemy is one step behind them. Knowing how they think is two steps ahead. The mindset of a progressive is that people DO NOT have the ability to think for themselves.

They look at us as a whole and put us all in the same category. They believe people are nothing more than stupid, greedy, and violent beings that can be manipulated. They believe that they have somehow been enlightened while we are all left in the dark to follow those who lead, and that our Founders' beliefs and the Constitution are outdated. They believe that people should be considered nothing more than machines that are good for nothing and should be used solely for contributions to society. Many people adore George Bernard Shaw for his plays and his influence in the world of theatre, but many people don't know the real Shaw himself. A Dangerous Progressive, Playwright George Bernard Shaw, once said, *"You must all know half a dozen people at least who are no use in this world, who are more trouble than they are worth. Just put them there and say, 'Sir, or Madam, now will you be kind enough to justify your existence?' If you can't justify your existence, if you're not pulling your weight in the social boat, if you're not producing as much as you consume or perhaps a little more, then, clearly, we cannot use the organizations of our society for the purpose of keeping you alive, because your life does not benefit us and it can't be of very much use to yourself."* Progressives are about "progress" and if you aren't contributing to or supporting their warped idea of progress, they believe your life has no meaning. Hmm... doesn't that sound a lot like *communism*? They believe that anyone who isn't condoning their beliefs, is in the dark, and it is up to them to "progress" forward.

Well, the last time I checked, progressives are human too. I suppose Nancy Pelosi's a bit questionable because of all those "operations." But other than her, progressives are just as human. However, because they believe differently, they already have plans set in place to accomplish their goals. The plan of progressives doesn't go deep into complexity and can be broken down easily to anyone willing to pay attention to their actions. All it's about is a "top down, bottom up" movement. Just ask Van Jones (former Green Jobs czar).

All it's centered around is the control of the media and the collapsing of a system, sending the people (citizens) running up, and sending the top (government) down with an "answer." Unbeknownst to the people going up, the top coming down has been corrupted by the ideals of progressivism. They want to make us think that everything they are doing is what's best for us, and that government interference in our everyday life is the best possible solution. The founders believed otherwise. THEY believed that the best answer to America's problem is for the people to educate themselves and question. Question EVERYTHING.

Question any move that is made by the government and ANYTHING you are told by ANYONE. That includes me. Please don't close your mind off to anything until you research, but always, ALWAYS research. When it comes to the game of Government, we've been left with no choice. But we can restore honor again. All you have to do is be willing to be the one who stands for it. First, check yourself, make sure you are based morally, and then question everything. Educate yourself, and source your information. And finally, speak with peace, boldness, and the truth. The role of Government is to sit in the dugout, and offer support when necessary. There is a fine line between supporting and doing the job for us, and progressives are using an Overton Window to dim that line.

The term 'Overton Window' originated from the mind of a man named Joseph Overton, former VP of the Mackinac Center. An Overton Window is a theoretical window in a range of public reaction to a certain idea or political concept. It works by moving the range of public acceptance to an idea toward one extreme or the other in order to make ideas previously thought of as radical or unthinkable, appear sensible or acceptable over time. Basically, if someone pushes a crazy idea long enough, but ever so delicately so as to not raise the public's eye, eventually people will accept it as part of every day society. This is around us every day. Think back to times of slavery or back before women were able to vote. Now we know better. Women and black people have and deserve the same rights as white males. But back then, the idea that black people could vote, own property, or work the same jobs as white people was crazy, as well as the idea that women could vote. But that's just an example.

The Overton Window of progressivism is slowly turning the idea that it's ok for government to do our thinking, or handle our bank accounts and health insurance, into acceptable behavior when it's not, especially considering all the problems that come with government. You're much better off thinking for yourself.

Progressives believe that if you DO think for yourself, but you don't believe exactly as they do, that you are dangerous and provocative to violence. They consider you a threat. It's almost laughable, because if you are someone who is able to depict the difference between right and wrong, and doesn't condone or base your strategy on violence, but ALSO doesn't condone the actions of the progressive movement, then you are considered a threat to their agenda, and progressives make you out to be someone who wants to destroy the country, rather than save it. They turn the nation's eye to demonize you because of violent acts, all the while people who really ARE committing violent acts are running amok in the streets with the public eye turned away. I'll put it this way: Progressives turn you into the leather, obnoxious motorcycle pants worn by old men when a mid-life crisis hits, which can't help but catch attention. All the while, they are the road-kill-resembling toupee on that old man's head. Little does everyone know, while they're occupied, staring at the obnoxious crotch riders, something even worse rests at the top.

The media today isn't too good at its job. See, its JOB is to report the truth. There are some out there who do this, but lately there are way too many people in the media who are only out to report one side. If something doesn't fit their script, they ignore it. It's as true today as it was back then. Reality doesn't match up with the reports we are getting. The overwhelming amount of one-sidedness, willful ignorance, and political games played by today's progressives and the media is staggering. Let me give you an example through the eyes of history. Martin Luther King Jr. was one of the most peacefully grounded men in the history of civil rights. We all know that. If you don't, you really do need to move out from under that rock. He received the Nobel Peace Prize in 1964 (you know, back when it actually meant something prestigious).

However, throughout his peaceful fight of enlightenment to the American public, he was somehow demonized by the media and blamed for violent rhetoric and rioting. On July 18 of 1966, The ***Tuscaloosa News*** reports, *"Responsible people in Chicago have accused King, and/or his staff members, of stimulating violence of the type which led to rioting. The charge is a valid one."*

King was a co-pastor to his father, at their church, Ebenezer Baptist, in Atlanta. He then became a HEAD pastor at the church, Dexter Avenue in Alabama. In 1957, he was elected president of the Southern Christian Leadership Conference. He based the principles of this organization from Christianity, and its operational approach from Gandhi. Everywhere he went, he went where there was injustice, and violence, and he preached peace and conscience. So tell me, does a man like that sound like someone who was paving the way for violence? No, I didn't think so either. Still, he was demonized by the media for doing things, not only did he not do, but for things he, in all actuality, hated.

All the while there were people like Malcolm X, William Ayers, and the Black Panthers group who not only condoned but maliciously executed the shooting of police officers, and were doing exactly what the media was attacking King for. So why would they go after King? Because King is founded solely on peace, the truth, and enlightenment, and unlike violence, that goes a long way. He was a real threat to their hidden agenda. See, violence eventually gets forgotten. A real difference is made by someone who refuses to give in to falsehoods, and remains hinged to their honor, integrity, and by what they know is true.

Who killed Gandhi? Do you know? We don't remember that guy as much as we do Gandhi, because Gandhi was about peace, and truthfulness which is why he was able to gain the independence of India. Those people who caused violence existed, but were ignored because they weren't a threat to anyone's selfish agenda. They were about vitriol, but King was about the truth. The truth is a threat because if everyone knew what was going on backstage, the play on stage would be ruined. So, the only truth they want you to know is their perverse version.

On January 8, 2011, a twenty two year old man named Jared Loughner, shot nineteen people at an open meeting led by U.S. Representative Gabrielle Giffords. He also shot Giffords herself, in the head. There was no doubt that this was a national tragedy incited by an insane young man. Much like the moments in our nation I spoke of in chapter five, this is a day that should be memorialized, rather than something we play politics with. But, what did the media do with this day? They blamed the actions of a psychopath on people such as Glenn Beck, Sarah Palin, and Rush Limbaugh. Rather than speaking of this day as it should be, with reverence and respect, the first thing they did was play the political game.

Progressives today are perverting the truth in an attempt to silence people, and hide anything that tells us the real truth. On January 16, 2011, a memorial conference was held for the Arizona shooting, filmed by the ***ABC*** broadcasting company called, ***"After the Tragedy: an American Conversation Continues."*** During the conference, Tucson Tea Party CO-Founder Trent Humphries was talking to the crowd about how, instead of clapping or parading, the meeting should be about reverence and memoriam. While he was talking, a progressive shooting survivor in the crowd named James Eric Fuller held up a picture of Humphries and said, "You're dead."

What did ABC do? They didn't point their cameras at him, or even have him QUIETLY excused from the meeting by security. They ignored it, and swept it under the rug. After the meeting, Fuller was taken into custody (8). According to some news reports, Fuller has apologized, so to stay on the safe side, let's just say he has. Even if it's true, trust me, there are still plenty of things to say about this froot loop. Still, doesn't that sound like the kind of violent rhetoric that today's progressives are accusing the people of, who believe contrary to them?

See, the progressive game works in a really twisted way. They believe that while people are stupid, there are still those people who "get out of the stupidity line" from time to time, and start speaking out. Then all of a sudden, these people need to be stopped and silenced because it doesn't fit their mindset, so they start accusing these people of vitriol and hate speech, demeaning anyone who stands against them. All the while, THEY are the ones condoning violence, and trying to silence anyone from speaking the truth. It's sick and controlling in nature, this game. If anyone incites violence, it's the progressive party.

If you need proof of that go back and read that story again about the twisted J. Eric Fuller. Ever heard of a progressive news research and information website called MediaMatters? They are a "non-profit" organization, barely, considering they have received with open arms large endorsements from powerful progressive leaders like George Soros whose funds (along with Hillary Clinton's) STARTED the program back in May of 2004. This news site does not report, it distorts the truth and seeks to silence. Their job as they've presented so far, is to tear apart the findings of news corporations including FOX News, and it's associates, such as Bill O'Reilly, Glenn Beck, and other conservative news industries like Rush Limbaugh in order to silence what they find as an opposing viewpoint. They aren't reporting error, they are solely stating and distorting what they disagree with. See for yourself, don't listen to me. Visit their site, and just look at their news. 99.7% of their articles are all about silencing FOX. They are even running a campaign called ***Drop FOX***.

Whether or not you agree with the FOX news

corporation, freedom of speech is an important right we all hold as individuals. I believe everyone has a right to their opinion, and that's why you can say anything on the floor of congress, and not be arrested for it, because we need differences of opinion. That is on another note, however. Media Matters recently ran an article entitled, "***Arizona Shooting Victim Criticizes Palin, Beck, and FOX News.***" In the article, they continually quote and condone the speech of J. Eric Fuller. You know, the crazy guy who threatened to kill a tea partier? In it, they don't mention his death threat. No, instead, they quote him on things he says such as, "*Sarah Palin doesn't bother to learn the spelling of repudiate and tosses out 'blood libel' like it was a jar of peanut butter, but does she know anything? -Probably about as much as (former Gifford's opponent) Jesse Kelly.*

"Let's say through some fluke Jared Loughner never ever heard of Sarah Palin or Beck or Rush Limbaugh or Sean Hannity and the rest of the crime syndicate, and dreamed it all up on his own, that he'd go over there and wack her. There are still plenty of demented people that are in need of a good spanking who are out there and plenty of access with the gun shops to assault weapons thanks to the son of privilege letting that expire. There is the matter of the media attention to it. It is going to make this even more desirable yet. If you are going to scream hatred and preach hatred, you're going to sow it after a while if you've got a soap box like they've got. We've got a surplus of demented dingbats, and wackos."

Fuller was then asked that if he had been requested, would he have likely appeared on FOX. He answered with this: "*I am afraid that might develop into a screaming session because I think they promote the war. I think I ought to pass on that, talking to Fox, I don't like what they're selling. I would stand up and just scream 'whores' at them, with my leg bleeding, and shock and with the congress lady laying on the pavement after having a slug pass through her head. I know they're just going to attack, they would probably attack me. They'll distort. Particularly Miss Blood Libel herself. The spoiled princess party. I am willing to take them on. I want to call them out and see if they have a peep to say."*

Well, Mr. Fuller, I have a peep to say. If anyone is promoting any type of war, it's you. And the type of war you're promoting isn't fought overseas. You are suggesting a war on our own soil, between brothers and sisters. It's sick, and while I would stand against anyone for your right to speak your mind, you and your words are an embarrassment to the American public. These words, HIS WORDS are the hate speech he, and progressives like him, are continually accusing people of. If anyone is dangerous, it's him. However, he has a right to say it. Sick, and misguided as it may be. If there is anyone out there condoning the vitriolic acts of violence, it's the progressive party. Stop looking, and waiting around for FOX news or CNN to say something violent, and research for yourself. Start listening to the words of people on the progressive march, like Frances Fox Piven, a 73 year old columnist for the magazine, "***The Nation.***" Look at some of the words of her article entitled, "***Mobilizing the Jobless.***" She calls for violence. In fact, she calls for riots in the streets, the same kinds that are happening in Greece and in Europe.

"So where are the angry crowds, the demonstrations, sit-ins and unruly mobs? After all, the injustice is apparent. Working people are losing their homes and their pensions while robber-baron CEOs report renewed profits and windfall bonuses. Shouldn't the unemployed be on the march? Why aren't they demanding enhanced safety net protections and big initiatives to generate jobs?"

Piven goes on, *"Mass protests might change the president's posture if they succeeded in pressing him hard from his base, something that hasn't happened so far in this administration. But there are obstructions to mobilizing the unemployed that would have to be overcome."*

Is it just me, or is she suggesting a riot against the White House??... Hmm, maybe I'm misreading. Let's allow her to try and explain, *"This problem of bringing people of different ethnicities or educational levels or races together is the classic organizing problem, and it can sometimes be solved by good organizers and smart tactics, as it repeatedly was in efforts to unionize the mass production industries. Note also that only recently the prisoners in at least seven different facilities in the Georgia state penitentiary system managed to stage coordinated protests using only the cell phones they'd bought from guards."*

Ok, I'm pretty sure I just noticed her suggesting that a riot ought to be as "persuading" as one is a prison. Hmm, well let's give her a chance. Who knows, maybe it was a typo. She also goes on to say, *"before people can mobilize for collective action, they have to develop a proud and angry identity and a set of claims that go with that identity. They have to go from being hurt and ashamed to being angry and indignant.*

"Protesters need targets, preferably local and accessible ones capable of making some kind of response to angry demands. This is, I think, the most difficult of the strategy problems that have to be resolved if a movement of the unemployed is to arise. Protests among the unemployed will inevitably be local, just because that's where people are and where they construct solidarities. But local and state governments are strapped for funds and are laying off workers.

"The initiatives that would be responsive to the needs of

the unemployed will require federal action. Local protests have to accumulate and spread—and become more disruptive—to create serious pressures on national politicians. An effective movement of the unemployed will have to look something like the strikes and riots that have spread across Greece in response to the austerity measures forced on the Greek government by the European Union, or like the student protests that recently spread with lightning speed across England in response to the prospect of greatly increased school fees."

Has she SEEN Greece or Europe during their riots? Have you? If not, let me inform you that People are over there DYING, law enforcement offices, OFFICERS, and banks are being set on fire, and some people are too scared to even leave their homes. She concludes in saying, *"A loose and spontaneous movement of this sort could emerge. It is made more likely because unemployment rates are especially high among younger workers. Protests by the unemployed led by young workers and by students, who face a future of joblessness, just might become large enough and disruptive enough to have an impact in Washington. There is no science that predicts eruption of protest movements. Who expected the angry street mobs in Athens or the protests by British students? Who indeed predicted the strike movement that began in the United States in 1934, or the civil rights demonstrations that spread across the South in the early 1960s? We should hope for another American social movement from the bottom—and then join it."*

History repeats itself. She is as plain as day when saying this, much as Woodrow Wilson was in his speech in Pennsylvania 1912. Much like I am laying out the steps to solve America's morality deficit, she is laying out steps to start a movement also. The key difference is my movement is by peaceful means of freedom and involves simply: Education, principles, and the truth. Her movement is one regarding the venomous uprising of people across the U.S.

The question is, now that you know the truth, now that you've learned from history, are you going to act on it? Let's get one thing straight, I am not solely targeting the progressives above because I disagree with them, even though I do ... wildly. I am simply speaking the truth. I do not hate progressives, nor do I want to see them caught in the crosshairs of any kind of violent act. On the contrary, I wish to see them stand for something honorable. If I saw that, I would stand along with them and fight for the good of the country. But until I do, I will continue to tell the truth, and consider them domestic enemies to the Constitution. I will not fight them, and I will not incite nor condone any type of violence upon them.

I will however, always speak the truth, whether that be against them or not. As long as Keith Olbermann is publicly referring to any United States citizen as a *"Poor, dumb manipulated bastard,"* I WILL speak the truth against the progressive cancer. That is the solution to this problem. I implore you to stand with me in all of these aspects. Your solution is simple. Do not allow people to silence you. Speak with compassion, responsibility, peace, truth, and speak against violence.

Reject anyone condoning violence. Whether they consider themselves from the left, or the right, if they are inciting acts of violence, like Frances Fox Piven, who is allegedly on the left, or the Neo- Nazi militia movement which is allegedly on the right, REJECT them, and instead of playing politics, speak out with peace, and boldness. It doesn't matter which side you come from; right, left, wherever. If you are inciting violence, I reject you. Like King, have truth on your side. Question everything you are told, enlighten yourself with the truth, and then do not remain silent.

7
Political Un-Correctness

"Banning red ink is a reaction to years of children having nothing but red over their work and feeling demoralized."
-Shirley Clarke, Associate of the Institute of Education On the subject of the color of a teacher's grading pen

One day, I was sitting down with my grandfather who was going over some paper work. My grandfather pilots aircrafts for a living. He could tell you the in's and out's of every single aircraft, war machine, or carrier plane dating back to the 1920's. If it flies, my grandpa could take it apart, and put it back together again. He is very good at his job and takes it very seriously, which is why I was curious about why he was looking over his paper work and laughing like he had just heard Lady Gaga try to sound smart. I asked him what he was going over. It was an advisory of issues that operators of the Bombardier (an airline manufacturer) were having with the ERSB, also called the Eye Reference System Balls.

This ERSB is a tool mounted on the windshield of an aircraft, and used by the pilot to configure the best cockpit seat adjustment for flight. The tool helps the pilot find the optimal seat adjustment to where he can best see out of the front of the plane. After having the job of the ERSB explained to me, I was still having trouble seeing what was so funny. So, my grandpa let me read over the Advisory sheet:

BOMBARDIER

ADVISORY WIRE

RFB789-23-1980

DATE: MARCH 26, 2006 **PAGE 1 OF 2**

FROM: BOMBARDIER BUSINESS AIRCRAFT CUSTOMER SUPPORT

SUBJECT: Windshield mounted lighted eye reference system balls (ERSB) used for pilot orientation and optimal seat position

EFFECTIVITY: BD700-1A11 (9210 & SUBS)

PROBLEM: It has come to our attention that many operators in the field are misusing or are unfamiliar with the proper use of their balls. The intent of this **ADVISORY WIRE** is to provide operational information and clarify some common misconceptions regarding the ERSB.

HISTORY: The original ball system was developed by China Airlines Captain, Ting Ling to assist pilots with a reference seat position for low weather minimums or category III approaches. It should be noted that the first successful CAT III approach was completed with Ting Ling Balls. Captain Ling originally had balls of steel but due to the interference with the magnetic compass Captain Ling switched to brass balls. Today's balls are commonly made with synthetic material and can be equipped with various options to include lighting and chimes. BOMBARDIER has recently developed a ball system with a 3-ring chime called the Dingle Ball. Some operators have opted for the NBAA system, which is No Balls At All. Regardless of the system you have installed, it is important that each operator understand the proper maintenance and use of their balls.

OPERATIONAL ISSUES: It has been reported that many pilots are spending way too much time adjusting their balls during critical phases of flight. Sighting your balls should require only a single adjustment; excessive handling should be avoided to prevent distraction and mechanical wear. Once a position is selected, stick to it. Remember, your balls are only an aid; it doesn't require balls to fly an approach. Some operators have adopted a policy of no ball adjustment below 10,000 feet. For those operators with lighted balls, there are some considerations regarding CRM. The "Pilot Flying" when appropriate, should initiate the call "light my balls" the "Pilot Not Flying" should respond with "your balls are lit captain." Common terminology can help prevent errors.

LIMITATIONS:
–Minimum operating temperature -25C (prevents blue balls issue)
–Avoid high temperature +40C & high humidity (prevents sweaty balls)

MAINTENANCE: Your eye reference system balls (ERSB) require little maintenance. Occasional dusting of your balls or cleaning with a damp cloth should be all that is required. Do not use harsh detergents and avoid scratching your balls. Avoid touching your balls any more than absolutely necessary. If your balls need replacement or adjustment, we always recommend the use of a trained professional. You shouldn't allow your balls to be handled by just anyone.

FREQUENTLY ASKED QUESTIONS
MY MAINTENANCE TECH HAS SUGGESTED SHAVING OUR BALLS TO ACHIEVE MORE PRECISE ALIGNMENT; WILL THIS GIVE ME AN EDGE?
No, your balls were carefully designed and aligned during installation; any unauthorized modification will void your warranty.

I operate a GLEX for a major tobacco company and find that heavy smoking has covered my balls with tar and nicotine, what is the best way to remove this goo? Lightly scrape your balls with the BOMBARDIER **silicon ball scraping tool (SBST)** to remove the heaviest build up, then wipe with a damp cloth. Under no circumstances use steel wool on your balls.

Our GLEX is based in OMAN and exposed to high temperatures and strong sunlight other than the 45C temperature limit. Is there any damage being done to my balls from the UV rays of the sun? Your balls have been designed to endure many extreme conditions, but extended exposure to UV can cause your balls to become brittle and lose their shine. I would recommend the use of the BOMBARDIER **eye reference system ball sack (ERSBC)**. This specifically designed cover will protect your balls from the most extreme conditions.

I recently heard of a pilot losing his balls during an approach. Is this possible?
This is very unlikely. The balls are securely mounted and unless they have been exposed to excessive handling or abuse it would be nearly impossible for them to come loose and roll about the cockpit. I suggest this may be an urban legend.

Project Manager
Beneficial Balls Project
BOMBARDIER

In all seriousness, this is a true story. This is a legitimate piece of paperwork that my grandfather received, and I promise, I'm going somewhere with it. What does this have to do with anything in this book? Well, besides the fact that I just HAD to find a place for it, let me ask you a question. When you were reading the above, were you thinking about what you were actually reading about: The ERSB tool of an airplane? Or were you laughing at every little thing one could possibly take as something else. If you're anything like the rest of the population, we all know you chose the second one.

When you read that, instead of connecting it with what it really means, you connect it with something it isn't, something some would find completely inappropriate. It's an honest mistake, one of which, again, we've all been guilty of making at one point or another. But in today's society, we're making the same mistake, and we're allowing people in power to magnify this problem. By doing so, we are allowing them the opportunity to cancel out our freedom of speech.

This is another one of the biggest threats we face today as Americans, and as people: Political Correctness. If you don't already know, political correctness is a term that describes the act of avoiding specific subjects of discussion, words, or actions that could be "perceived" to exclude or "insult" people who are "socially disadvantaged" or "discriminated against."

Do you remember that term, "Overton window?" While the definition sounds nice and friendly, longing for nothing but "fairness," political correctness today is the mother ship of Overton Windows. Today, political correctness has been used as a massive defense strategy for the government's obsessive control tirade over our rights as individuals. Political Correctness, much like progressivism, has its own sketchy past, and originated from, who would have guessed? Communism.

Georg Lukacs was the Deputy Commissioner for culture in the Bolshevik Bela Kun Regime in Hungary in 1919. Never heard of it? Yeah, I figured. That's because Lukacs' plans for "culture" made the regime extremely short-lived. His plans were to rip the Christian religion and lifestyle out of Hungary (Again, who does that remind me of?) Lukacs launched a radical sex education program in schools which taught the younger generation how to live out "free love" which is politically correct for Robert Downy Jr. on a good day. Basically, having loads and loads of sex is "alright." The youth were tutored graphically in sexual intercourse all the while being taught to reject the Christian faith along with any ethics that came along with it. Which means, it didn't take long for the society to turn inside out, and bring up a massive generation of rapists and serial killers.

Because this regime was so short-lived, Lukacs needed new ground to cover. So he extended his plans in an attempt to spread his newfound "multiculturalism" over here to the west in an attempt to take out what he considered a roadblock to communism: Our culture. In 1923, a Marxist think-tank known as Frankfurt School was started from The "Institut fur Sozialforschung" or Institute of Social Research (ISR) in Germany. Among the founders of this were Lukacs himself, as well as Herbert Marcuse (who created the 'Make love, not war' phrase from the Vietnamese war period), and Theodore Adorno. The idea of this think-tank was to mix together the ideas of all three men, which included: Lukacs' idea of "free love," psychoanalysis conditioning techniques, and Marcuse's idea of polymorphous perversion.

This newfound cultural terrorism expanded with Theodore Adorno's idea of "Authoritarian" personality. This idea's concept is that Christian ethics, the second amendment, or capitalism would cause a child to be raised in a way that would be racist or fascist, and that anyone who believes in basic morality, tradition of family, and humanistic values needs therapeutic help. Lukacs and his cohorts also believed that the Christian ethics and freedom loving virtues of the west were the obstacles keeping their communist "new world order" in the dark, and that for their dream to go anywhere, the west (us) must first be conquered.

I don't know though, it doesn't sound like nearly as much fun as concentration camps, gulag strings, shared wealth, and all the OTHER fantastic ideas that branched from communism. When Hitler took over, with the help of Columbia University, the ISR fled from Germany to New York City in 1933. When they arrived, they continued spreading their multiculturalism in the U.S. and their plan to conquer and reconstruct our culture is still being executed successfully today by current organizations that you'll see pop up later.

Unlike the founding vision, in which everyone is considered equal with a fair chance to live just as well as the next person, the idea of multiculturalism is that all history is dictated by the power that specific ethnicities, or groups hold over other groups. For example, some races are considered "victims of circumstance," regardless of any wrong they may commit, while others who believe, say, in free speech, Christianity, or capitalism are regarded as racists, fascists, or homophobes. Those Politically Correct do not condone nor believe in the right to speak freely. They believe words must be "controlled" in order to keep other races or groups of people from being offended.

Like I said, most people who have fallen under the politically correct category are just making an honest mistake. MOST of them actually have the best interests at heart when it comes to keeping people happy, they just aren't thinking about who they might be offending - like the people they are "defending" in the fight to "protect." Do you think you're helping a person living in poverty if all you're doing is arguing over how to correctly refer to them? Don't you think they would be more offended by that than anything? There are still those who use it to try and fade out America's culture and replace it with one under communism. The really sad part about this is that this Overton Window is so vast, and has been drug on for so long, that unlike back in the 1950's, communists are no longer afraid to show their faces in the country.

Way back during the Cold War, after WWII, there was an eruption of fear from the people in the United States known as a second Red Scare, which was fear that communism may have been infiltrating the U.S. Back then, people in the U.S. were extremely prejudiced toward the idea of communism. An organization was established, called the House Committee of Un-American Activity (HUAC), and in September, 1947, it subpoenaed 43 witnesses to attest to the cases against individuals for communism in Hollywood. We were arresting and trying people who were found to be communists.

The First Red Scare actually originated after the WWI armistice was executed in 1918, which called for cessation of fighting along the western front, in an attempt to keep communism from spreading to the U.S. or any other nations. Socialist groups became prone to attack, and were the centerpiece of American suspicion because of their opposition to WWI. On September 9, 1919, the Boston police force went on strike, and panic took over, with the belief that communism was behind it. This resulted in civil unrest, and fear that commies were spreading throughout the nation.

Even after the strikes ended in January of 1920, without the compliance of any demands, the force was branded communist, and "Red Hunting" became the nation's top priority. The Red Scare even made it up to state legislatures with multiple ordinances being passed in a number of states against radical activity, some even restricting the possession, or showing of the red communist flag. On January 2, 1920, over 4,000 people were arrested in thirty three cities for being alleged radicals, and were tried in court. In 1945, a foreign policy of containment in the U.S. was passed in an attempt to control the spread of communism.

Now, are some of these ideas and punishments too extreme? Yes, very much so. But communism is not American and way back when, people who were viewed as communists were imprisoned because the threat of communism was recognized. Nowadays, we are blind to it's dangers. It's astounding how far we've come since then. People were blacklisted and put in prison to be tried for even associating with communism. Today, communists are openly coming out and are unafraid. Why? Because they see their plan of expansion is working.

They see that we are asleep, so they no longer fear discrimination, or discrepancies. If you need proof of that, just go to their WEBSITE, the Communist party of America, www.cpusa.org. It will tell you everything about the communist party that they think you should be allowed to know. On facebook.com, the Communist Party of America has its own page with more than 6,000 fans. They are coming out, no longer hiding, but for the moment, still trying to hide their agenda for the country.

Political Correctness is a threat to the U.S., because while some people condone it without being informed and the best interest in their heart, some do not. They only aim to strap down the right of free speech granted to us by God and founded in the roots of America. I think people living in poverty would be more offended by the fact that we're fighting over what to refer to them as, rather than how to stop it. Like the progressives' agenda, political correctness aims to restrict speech, which is one of the things this country so desperately needs again. But, political correctness goes even further than restricting. It distorts the meaning of people's words or the meaning of a symbol.

It's even spread to the school system. America has seen a largely increasing number of school teachers changing the color of their grading pen from classic red to something a little less (try to hold in your laughter) "frightening." Umm....really? This whole idea began in the U.K., and in Australia, but eventually somehow made its way over here. Research shows that some teachers in the U.S. have come to the belief that the color red is aggressive in appearance and "makes the children feel as if they've done something wrong." I think I've been in school long enough to know that if there's red on my paper, I DID get something wrong.

Red is not aggressive, it's a COLOR. Sure it's been associated over the years with certain bad aspects, but so have other colors. This isn't worrying about children; this is being trivial in the world of education - and we wonder why China is beating out our students in graduation statistics and test scores. Because we're too focused on making our kids "comfortable," it's blinding us to real issues. The point is, if you change the color from red to something like blue, or green, eventually we'll start associating THOSE colors with aggression and insensitivity.

If we start playing this game with kids, it isn't going to prepare them for anything, and the last time I checked that's what school was for; preparation for the real world. If we're worried about not hurting their feelings, how are we preparing them for anything in the future? Because I guarantee the real world isn't half as worried about being sensitive. Sure, the idea behind not focusing on what kids did wrong and more so what they did right is nice, but it isn't realistic and cannot be how the educational system is run.

I'm all for letting kids believe in themselves and letting them know that they can do anything they set their mind to. Heck, if I hadn't gotten that from my parents as a kid, I probably wouldn't have even written this. But what I also got was the chance to fail. And WHEN I failed, I was told flat out what needs to be fixed and what I need to improve on. That is a vital part of childhood. Without that step, we allow our children to grow up unprepared for failure and, even worse, uninformed as to what to do with failure.

Political correctness targets so much more than just the trivial color of a grading pen. According to a survey in England, some teachers no longer teach about the Holocaust because it offends Muslim students. In Washington 2010, Governor Chris Gregoire once refused to allow a nativity scene at Christmas time near the state capitol because her attorneys did not have an allotted amount of time to "research the matter." In 2005, the ACLU (American Civil Liberties Union) targeted the University of Illinois and their mascot for "offensive use of American Indian imagery."

At the University's home game, their mascot would dress as a Native American and perform an Indian dance ritual at half time. The ACLU then went on a ban spree against high schools and colleges across the U.S. whose team or mascot names were connected with anything Native American. They eventually lost in court, having to reverse their ban, when the Seminole Indian tribe teamed up with Florida State.

Oh, but I'll give this to them; the ACLU doesn't give up. They're latest attack targeted a company called Chick-fil-A, founded by S. Truett Cathy and led by current president Dan T. Cathy, for "gay-hating." The agency is targeting the Company for no other reason than donating refreshments to a conservative conference at the Pennsylvania Family Institute called "The Art of Marriage: Getting to the heart of God's design." I oppose anyone who is out there screaming hatred toward anyone, but this company is at no fault. In fact, this company is founded on morality and integrity and has never claimed to hate anyone regardless of race, religion, or belief. The ACLU has just gotten personal, because I have worked at a Chick-fil-A in my home state. Chick-fil-A is a company founded on faith, integrity and honor. If the ACLU wants to get to them just for the sake of sucking money out of innocent people for their own gain, they're gonna have to come through me first. So please ACLU, I dare you, come and get me.

In 2010, the TSA (Transportation Security Administration) which is in charge of national Airport security enacted new X-ray systems in airports across the nation that literally scanned underneath a person's clothing invading their personal space. What's even worse is that the images are allegedly stored in the security's database, according to an article by Chief Political Correspondent of CNET, Declan McCullagh. However, passengers could opt out of the x-ray, instead receiving a violating pat down.

But, don't worry, according to the TSA, its "all for your safety." Oh. Ok, well then I guess it's alright for you to touch my grandma like that, officer. Does that make any sense to you? They want to crack down for safety, but they also want to be inclusive and not offend anyone, so instead of searching only those under suspicion, they just do it to everyone. What really frosts me on this subject, is that Muslim passengers get special privileges when it comes to opting out of these searches. Who's being inclusive here? Don't blame the officers for doing the searches; they're just doing their jobs. I honestly don't think they enjoy it anymore than we do. Political correctness is beginning to eat away at common sense.

The problem with current organizations like the ACLU, is that they claim to be all for spreading "inclusiveness" and indoctrinating "fairness," when all they really want is to break down what they see as an obstacle to their agenda: American Culture. Don't you think it's weird how we can connect this issue with every other problem we face in the country? It's because all the issues are being caused by the same people in power. It's all connected. The solution to this issue isn't an easy one, but it is possible. It involves the resurrection of one of my long lost friends, whom I miss too much to keep away anymore: Common sense.

The problem isn't the words or symbols that we're using. The problem is that WE are giving them the power to be offensive and dangerous. Red is just another color, its only dangerous if we make it that way. We're allowing words to control us, and it's a big part of what is killing us. Over the last year, the website www.youtube.com has seen more video uploads of public displays of violence than ever before. What was the Governments solution? Well, start controlling what is uploaded to the internet, of course. Let's get one thing straight. WE are the problem, not the website, and not the words. Free speech is under constant threat every day by the current administration. The Media and people like Ms. Nancy Pelosi, and Mrs. Hillary Clinton, her husband and even President Obama jump at every chance they have to try and silence a differing of opinion.

Until people decide to stop giving these things the power to control us, we can't fix our broken union. What kind of corrupt society do we live in when a high school student can't confide in a teacher about his choice of abstinence without being called to the office for a sexual harassment charge, without being approached about it first? But idiots like Tucker Max can publish 300-page, graphically detailed vulgar books about nothing but getting wasted and having sex with as many girls as possible. Or when we start treating airline passengers like cheap porn stars, instead of paying passengers. Political Correctness has a stranglehold on American society and the solution is simple: Stop being so spoiled with the idea of free speech.

It's time to start realizing that this freedom is under attack, and that we need to start fighting for it by using it the right way: The way the founders intended, not Marxists. When we give in to politically correct ideals, we give way to an attack on our American voice, opinions, beliefs, and on common sense itself. The more we give certain groups a reason to believe that they have the ability to have their way, wherever and whenever, the more some people will take advantage of that. If you want inclusiveness, then BE inclusive. Don't make one group higher than another because of their "special personality." That isn't inclusiveness, that's favoritism, and we get enough of that from today's Administration.

Sure, inclusiveness is a cute idea, and is acceptable to an extent. But, this is a country of diversity, and the only way to get that is by allowing common sense, and all sorts of different viewpoints on the table, regardless of how misinformed, or ignorant they may be. Choose to be someone who speaks with responsibility, truth, and honor. Stop sweating the small stuff and playing the party game and start having real debates, real arguments, and real UNREGULATED conversations. Realize that part of what makes us America is the right to speak and believe what we choose. No amount of government regulation can change that.

8

Faith, Speech, Integrity, And Other "Old News"

"I hope I shall possess firmness and virtue enough to maintain what I consider the most enviable of all titles: the character of an honest man."
-George Washington

When you hear someone talking about how "poor we are as a country," what's the first thing that springs to your mind? Do you think about the mountains and MOUNTAINS of monetized debt of a continually growing $14 trillion? Or, how about the fact that if we were to give every U.S. citizen a chunk of the debt, each man, woman, and child would receive approximately $45,148 and rising. By the way, that's enough to purchase each man, woman and child a trip around the world three times. Oh, here's a good one, how about the rising U.S. debt of $4,464,767,400,000 owed to foreign countries like China?

Well, I'll tell you what I think about. The first thing that comes to my mind is the major deficit of morality, and integrity the American population is facing. On top of the piling debt we are under, that is where we are the poorest; because before we have the ability to fix our debt and deficit problem, we must first fix the problems within ourselves.

People today are not back-checking anything that is going on in Washington. They are taking the administration's word for everything that is passed, and any action that's taken, and that's a big problem considering people in power today are more worried about satisfying their hungry pockets than protecting the greater good of the nation. Even some, who do know what's going on, don't believe there's anything they can do, so they remain silent. That's a big problem, because as we remain silent, corruption expands from underneath us.

In 2009, Federal Reserve Inspector General Elizabeth A. Coleman, was questioned by former House Representative Alan Grayson, in a federal court about the identity of the recipients of an unaccounted-for amount of $1trillion. Her response to said question was, and keep in mind this is the Inspector GENERAL of the FEDERAL RESERVE, *"I do not. No, we have not looked at that ... specific area."* She was also asked what the Federal Reserve has done to investigate its losses which totaled $9 trillion in the past eight months. Her response, after dancing around the question, was, *"At this point, we are conducting our lending facility project at a fairly high level, and have not gotten to a specific level of detail to really be in a position to respond to your question."* Let me get this straight ... Is the Inspector GENERAL of the FEDERAL RESERVE OF THE U.S. saying that no one at the federal reserve is keeping track of the money its "misplacing?" The disease of corruption is overthrowing common sense and decency in Washington. We are laying back, allowing principles and our freedoms to be taken from us, and buying into every excuse in the book from political pundits as to why certain rights are "inapplicable" in today's society.

Most Americans aren't doing this–in spite of the country–they just don't know what to do about it. They're unsure what the answer is, but all they know is that there is SOMETHING wrong. What's wrong is that there is a structure being built. A structure that cannot be put into effect until the old structure of the United States is taken down, and the corrupt in power know exactly what they need to do.

In order to accomplish that. All the elitist movement of today needs is a massive collapse of what they believe is the previous system of America. Raise the debt to an all time high, collapse the idea of old principle, and individual enterprise, devalue the U.S. currency to an almost worthless state, and people will look to and trust anyone who claims they have the answer. Some people are already playing into this progressive idea of "top down-bottom up," meaning they're looking to the Government for an answer. The problem is the "top down" part, because the government today is no longer run on integrity, freedom, or the best interests of the people. It is run by a thirst for power, and the ideal of an expanding government (which as you know from the last few chapters is a bad idea) and hungry federal pocketbooks.

Debt is not a bad thing. When you have a healthy financial plan along with a manageable debt, on a few moderate necessities, it's just part of the financial cycle. However, when we start selling our nation's culture and soul away to other countries like China, for the sake of printing more money and gaining more and more excess, I think it's a safe bet to say we're headed down a pretty dangerous road. One that could ultimately destroy us if not veered from in time. It's when you start living in and off the debt that puts you on a path headed for financial and economic ruin, and that's how our administration and today's government is driving us toward fiscal suicide.

That is why we cannot leave the answer up to Washington. The answer lies with the people of a nation, and the founders knew that. Which is why they set the U.S. up to work the way it does. The government plays only as an aid when absolutely needed. When people who have the ability to work, choose instead to take handouts from the government, and the government continues to hand it out from unknown locations, and from the pocket of hard working U.S. citizens, that is when we are officially pushing ourselves over a cliff of collapse. Part of this problem is our faith; the kind of faith that you hold for your country, and your country's future, and its leaders.

We have lost that faith, and any ideal connected with it. Many of us in the nation have lost faith in the future of America. We've given up, fallen asleep and left the ruins to be reconstructed by the elite corrupt in Washington. We have no more faith in our leaders. Today's popular belief is that most people affiliated with the world of politicians are corrupt liars. That's our first instinct today as a nation when it comes to political leaders. Is that what faith is considered to be in today's society?

Faith was a founding cornerstone of this country in more than one aspect. While the founders leaned on and stood strictly by faith in God, they also leaned on their faith in the people and the goodness and morality that is sewn into the fabric of our hearts naturally. Against the ideals of progressivism, I believe as my founders did: That people are not violently manipulated knuckle-dragging statistics, but that they are beings born with a conscience and the ability to depict the difference between right and wrong. They are born with the ability to think for themselves, learn and adapt, and are endowed with certain inalienable rights granted by God, which include the right to liberty, life, and the pursuit of happiness.

The elite today are trying to convince us that we are beings who need to be baby-sat, and led and controlled for the "good of the nation." But the American public is not stupid. We know the difference between right and wrong and falsehoods and truth. We go about our daily lives not paying any more than what we can afford, and using no more than what we've earned, and its just common sense to see to it that the government does the same.

The Nation was built to run on a document we know as the Constitution. The Constitution is a document that sets up the rights of a thinking body of people. It's funny how the bill for health care reform is several THOUSAND pages long, but the Constitution, the single document that maps out the rights of the people and a nation that would be considered one of the world's most prosperous is only FOUR pages of parchment paper. Why does the progressive party hold such a vindictive opinion of the U.S. Constitution? Because, it's goal is to limit the power of the government by giving the people of a nation the power.

The founders, when setting up their new government, knew they couldn't create a dictatorship because of all the corruption and previous failure that came along with it. They knew they didn't want a monarchy because that's what they were running from in the first place, and they wanted to avoid a democracy for the most part because it gave feelings and human emotion too much control in the world of debate. However, they still wanted to keep some of the ideals of democracy. So through the Constitution, they created a republic. A Representative Republic. One system that slowed things down just enough that all different viewpoints and aspects were put into the pot of ideas, and could be viewed, heard, revised, and produced accordingly. As I've said before, this idea of people not knowing how to control themselves isn't new, and extends all the way back to the birth of the nation.

Pop quiz time: Who was the first president of the United States? (Insert jeopardy theme song) If you answered George Washington, sorry, you're about seven presidents off. Washington was the first president under the Constitution that we follow today, but before we had the Constitution, we had something called the Articles of Confederation, after the Revolutionary war. The Articles were proposed in Congress on June 11, 1776, but not agreed upon until November 15, 1777.

Once the actual signing of the Articles took place in 1781, many in congress, including George Washington, unanimously chose a man named John Hanson as president because of his influence and his role in the previous revolution. The Articles only ran a president's term for one year and the role wasn't very well defined, seeing as no one had been in the position before. So Hanson had a big job ahead. He accomplished a lot in his one-year term. Hanson was actually the one who established the Great Seal of the United States, the first Secretary of War, Foreign Affairs Department, Treasury Department, and even the set date of Thanksgiving.

When Hanson's term ended, six men followed in his shoes. A man named Elias Boudinot in 1783, Thomas Mifflin in 1784, Richard Henry Lee in 1785, Nathan Gorman in 1786, Arthur St. Clair in 1787, and finally Cyrus Griffin in 1788. The Articles of Confederation did not accomplish the goal of the United States at all. It limited the government so much that business couldn't be done across state lines. They were too close to anarchy. The individual states couldn't agree on anything because they held too much of the power.

James Madison of Virginia had studied for years, the science behind politics and all the possible train wrecks America could face through economic dilemma. He saw the potential danger in having independent states. So during the year of 1785, James Madison and Thomas Jefferson of Virginia began proposing to each other the idea of a new system. One which the people controlled. They knew they couldn't pass on such a radical idea straight to congress because of a massive lack of trust at the time, due to the corruption across state lines. So they had to find someone they knew would present this new system the right way and who had the ability to bring everyone together. A man who would later be elected president of the Philadelphia Convention; George Washington. In 1787, the Articles were scrapped and we started over.

Some of the members of congress (known as the Anti-federalists) rejected the idea of this new Constitution because it gave too much power to the people themselves. However, through much debate, sweat and tears, the Constitution of the United States was signed on September 17, 1787. It lined up the faith that the founders had in America's people. It held the inalienable rights entrusted to the people through the individual ability to depict right and wrong, and to educate themselves in the way of common sense. Today, we're facing a deficit of faith. It's as if we've moved ourselves back under the rule of the Articles of Confederation, and established a new party of Anti-federalists.

We've allowed division among a once united nation through the nitpicking of words, and the materialism we've given away to the people in power. How do we unify a divided nation? Don't look around, or to the "top" for an answer. YOU are the answer. We unify ourselves the same way the founders did, by realizing that bigger government is the problem, and not the solution. The solution lies in the faith of the people in their leaders and neighbors. When we don't enlighten ourselves in society and in the politics and principles of the people we elect, then we become a part of one of our nation's killers; ignorance. We have the power, but if we don't use it wisely, the government today has no problem taking it from us.

Faith comes through questioning and thinking, which is why today if you question things, you're considered a threat. Free speech today has been Overton Windowed as sedition. It's been transformed into a game where American citizens are being pitted against each other because of differing opinions. We're buying into the lie that speaking your mind and heart makes you a hate monger.

Progressives in power want to make us believe that they are not the radical ones, but that the original fundamentals of America are what is radical. No one is standing up because a lot of people in the media today no longer want to tell the truth. We're facing an honesty shortage in America, not just with media, but with a lot of higher-ups and because of this, people are ignoring the real story. We need to realize that we have a duty to be honest when it comes to speaking our right. Speak with boldness and enlightenment and do not give in to the lie that you are the problem. YOU are the solution. When you realize that government has no right to take someone's well-earned money, and give it to someone else, and has no right to infiltrate your bank statements, personal life, or to decide whether or not someone should live or die, then you know common sense.

It's when you decide to do something with common sense that you become a threat to their agenda. When I say "do something," I don't mean rebelling and rioting, I mean speaking out. It's when you are no longer silent that you become trouble. Then you become the target of the trash talk of corrupt media and progressives all over the nation.

Take the Tea Party for instance. Media and political pundits all over the nation, such as Bill Clinton, are taking the actions of people like Oklahoma Bomber Timothy McVeigh, and comparing them to the actions of the Tea Party. Let me tell you what the Tea Party is. They aren't a group of racist militiamen bent on the destruction of all things government. They are regular working class people who are concerned about the survival of their nation given the economic downturn we face. They are concerned about the amount of America's soul that the Administration is selling away to other countries, and the amount of money it's giving out like candy when it has no idea where it's coming from or going to.

They are people concerned about their government's giving money to companies that can never pay it back, and how the government went behind closed doors and created a health care system that consists of thousands of pages, most of which remain to be read by even the crafters, and which has already been challenged in court for being unconstitutional. What's even stranger is that as much as he claims to believe in this "obamacare," President Barack Obama exempts twenty eight unions, leadership staff of the Senate and House who WROTE the bill, VP Mr. Joe Biden, close friends of the president, and his own family from having to take it. He has also, so far not given a logical reason as to why. You have to ask yourself, "If he thinks it's so great, why wouldn't he take it himself? Or give it to all his friends and comrades?" Think about it. Have you ever heard the phrase, "actions speak louder than words?" Are his words, that propose his health care bill he claims to love so much, matching up with his actions? No, and that's why people such as the Tea Party are standing up against it. The federal government cannot force people to purchase health care, or anything else. It IS Unconstitutional.

Tea Partiers are respectable, peaceful, working folk who refuse to be silent about the peril of their homeland or their family, and because of this, they are demonized by media attacks and progressives' verbal abuse around the country.

Since when is speaking the truth seditious? We are a country based on the idea of free speech. Silencing opinions doesn't help the country, it only hurts us. It puts us in a hole right along with socialism. The Tea Party is a group of all different races and political leniencies. It isn't the right or the left. It is just a group of people who understand what the answer is and are doing something about it. The answer lies in connected principles, such as faith, and unregulated speech. The answer to our problem does not lie in crying hate speech or saying only what you have to or want to, but speaking the whole truth. America is a nation built on the power of the individual. Not the power of kings, lords, or dictators, but the INDIVIDUAL. Tea partiers, legitimate tea partiers, are not nor have they ever portrayed the characteristics of radicals. Radicals, like communism and Nazism, will take America down a destructive new road if we sit by and allow them to do so. We need to realize that while they claim to believe different things, they in retrospect, are the same group. They aren't the republicans or the democrats. They have nothing to do with America, they are the progressive left and progressive right. They are both socialistic and they do not belong here.

How do I know that what the Tea party is doing is working? Because of how much the media and progressive movement are trying to silence them. We need to realize that through self education, discipline and integrity, we have the ability to take our rightful place in the nation, and replant ourselves in the vision of the founders. Through ridding ourselves of integrity, we have replaced it with being worried about ourselves and no one else. What is also dividing us so much is a sense of self preservation, in which we are playing directly into the hands of progressives and people of power.

As I've said, government's hostile takeover isn't a new idea, it's been around for a long time. It just hasn't been as magnified up until this point. During the Clinton Administration, the Department of Energy funded a study involving the research and remediation of six nuclear weapon sites, which would report to Congress those locations with the greatest risk to the public. Millions of dollars were spent and many meetings held at resorts and hotels without so much as a finger lifted to remediate a single risky location. My father and his partner were hired as Logistics Professionals for this CERE Project in 1994. He was an ear-witness to the "philosophy" of the ideals of expanding government control.

He was challenged on more than one occasion by the idea of the government's role in society, being told that if government had the control desired by some politicians, and progressives, then we wouldn't have to worry about all the people panhandling on the streets or have to worry about rejecting them when they ask for money. Is that what it's about? They want the government to babysit the public because they don't have the gall to say no to someone? I have a hard time walking away from someone on the streets who I see is in need of help, but the problem is that some of them don't need help at all. Some of them are only looking to receive a handout.

Well, how can you tell the difference? If someone on the street asks you for your help, instead of draining your wallet, offer to buy them something to eat or offer to buy them a room for the night. Or offer to drive them to the nearest shelter. If they say "no, that's alright, but I'd be glad to take the money," chances are they're probably just someone looking to be rewarded for not doing anything and they've probably got a nicer house and car than you. The problem with the government taking over is that they are giving these people the handouts they are asking for.

Charity should come from the heart, not the federal government. We, as a people, need to help those in need because our hearts are the only trustworthy place that charity comes from. When it comes from the heart, it's much more efficient, includes a lot more integrity, and we can get a lot more done - minus the fraud. It isn't the government's job to nanny us. Government aid is there when we absolutely need it. When people who have the ability to work but choose not to, start receiving money from the pocket of someone who's earned it, that's a BIG problem. That's not charity. That's socialism and stealing.

For every dollar that goes to the government to help people who need it, the government makes it a nickel. We are the ones who need to stand up and help those who really need it. If you have the ability to work, then work. And when you work, stand by your integrity and ethics, hold on to your well earned money, and never accept a handout. I implore you to help those who need it with sense and compassion in your heart.

The big picture is that the federal bureaucracy is putting

off principles founded and rooted in this country as the past, and that the future is much brighter with them in charge. They push that the time for individual enterprise, freedom of speech and thought, and individual charity is over. But through giving these up, we have also lost our faith in our leaders and our people. We've allowed them to silence us and reform our ideals to fit their agenda.

The reason we can't leave the answer to Washington is because the corporations and ideals they set forth aren't founded in humanity, but in selfishness, power, and even in some cases, the exact opposite of humanity. If you want to know the corruption of corporations with hidden agendas, such as the Planned Parenthood Federation of America, go back to the words of the person who founded them. Planned Parenthood was founded by a woman named Margaret Sanger in 1942.

This woman, in her time, wrote many books and spoke publicly about the subject of abortion and birth control. In her book, ***Women and the New Race***, she states that, *"The most merciful thing that a large family does to one of its infant members is to kill it."* Does that sound messed up to you too? This woman believed that children were to be nothing but thoroughbreds, and raised to be able to contribute to society. She hated the black population, immigrants, indigents, homeless people, and mentally or physically handicapped people. In her work, ***Pivot of Civilization***, she refers to these groups as, *"human weeds," "reckless breeders," and "human beings that should never have been born."*

This woman was one who believed that if one did not contribute enough to society, then they should be killed. She was a sick, disturbed woman. ALL human life has meaning. This woman's goal was to push population control and what greatly resembles Georg Lukacs' idea of "Free love." Do you remember how that turned out? A few of this woman's avid supporters, including Hillary Clinton, believe Sanger to be a hero somehow, and Planned Parenthood today follows the vision of their founder pretty closely.

Faye Wattleton, president, said in the ***LA Times*** on October 17, 1986, *"We are not going to be an organization promoting celibacy or chastity."* The last time I checked, that was the only sure way to prevent teenage pregnancy. The people of Planned Parenthood are willing to do "business" behind the backs of the minors' parents, as said by a representative who lectured students of Ramona High School in California on April 22, 1986. *"At Planned Parenthood you can also get birth control without the consent or knowledge of your parents. So, if you are fourteen, fifteen or sixteen and you come to Planned Parenthood, we won't tell your parents you've been there. We swear we won't tell your parents."*

Tell me why a decent number of projects and foundations including some museums, shelters, or even certain libraries are paid for by donation, volunteer work, and fundraising, while millions of tax dollars –YOUR money– is spent to keep the lights on for Planned Parenthood? Tell me something else: Is it just me, or is something wrong with the mindset that it's much more productive to use U.S. citizen tax dollars to fund the mass murder of infants, rather than to hold abstinence programs? Because, that's the exact idea that Planned Parenthood is based on, according to a letter from the Planned Parenthood of Hawaii CEO Barry Raff in 2007. He referred to abstinence programs as, "*dangerous,*" "*ineffective,*" and programs that "*just don't work.*" I don't know about the rest of the population in this fantasy world, but in the real world, abstinence has worked pretty well for me in preventing pregnancy. So I fail to see the danger that comes from teaching teens its benefits. Raff, referring to state abstinence programs, claims that *"One hundred million dollars are spent annually in the United States ($900,000 in Hawaii) that deny teenagers information to protect their health."* Wow, abstinence is bad for your health?

Let me do the math here. Unprotected sex is dangerous. I think we all agree on that. Protected sex is only ninety percent guaranteed with a ten percent margin of error. But, somehow, doing nothing is dangerous? With this study, I think I've come up with a new slogan for Planned Parenthood- "Demise of the unborn and poor math skills all in one package." Abstinence programs are only dangerous to the abortion industry pockets. Let's take a little ride down reality lane here, shall we? We know that statement is a load, because first off, of course, abstinence isn't bad for your health. Second off, even if the amount of 100 million American tax dollars IS going to fund abstinence programs, according to an article by CNS, a "fact sheet" published by Planned Parenthood themselves, shows that 349.6 million tax dollars had gone to Planned Parenthood by the end of June, 2008. By that date they had been able to perform 324,008 abortions, and pay their president, Cecille Richards $385,163, plus another $11,876 in benefits and compensations. Now, in my opinion, I don't believe that American tax dollars should go to fund either of these, especially not the amount that they are receiving. However, if you had to choose, which would you rather pay for: Classes teaching your kids the benefits of waiting until marriage for sex? Or a doctor who offers to kill your teenager's baby and has no problem keeping it from you and overcompensating their leader? Foundations such as Planned Parenthood or the Christianity hating ACLU are not the ones the solutions should be left to.

Charity is a term that has now been warped from a

humanistic value to Marxist propaganda. The transforming has weaseled its way into our courtrooms, our schools, and even our churches, cloaked in the politically correct disguise, "social Justice." Yes, God wants us to give to our neighbors, but that charity needs to come from our hearts, and not from the federal red, white and blue. The answers to restoring faith, integrity and charity in America lie in plain sight as our founders intended. The solution to fixing the nation is fixing the deficit of character first. Enlarging and magnifying the government to the point at which it is making our choices for us is not the answer. The answer lies in the principles rooted in the heart of the country. The principles and values of faith, integrity, humanity, and the freedom of speaking out aren't "old news," they're just dusty. All we have to do is embrace them once again and we can find the answer to anything our country faces economically, or morally. Prove to the people in power that the American public is not led by a price and cannot be controlled though materialism, or fear of collapse or threats. We are people and we cannot be bought. WE have the power.

We, the people, are where God and the founders intended the power to be cultivated. Not to make it a corny Spiderman moment, but with great power does come an even bigger responsibility, but that is where faith comes in. I have faith in the people of the United States. People are choosing sides, so make sure that you are on the right one. The system may fail but in the end, the truth never does. It is time to stand up for our republic while it's still alive, and stop playing games. It's time to stand up for honor.

9

Strength Of A Nation

"We don't remember those who fell apart, we remember those who stood strong when they could've fallen apart."
-Dr. Bryan Cutshall

Where does the strength of a nation lie? Does it lie with the amount of military personnel, or number of weapons, or nuclear advances it's made? Does it lie with the leader? All of those aspects can help or hurt the morale of the country, but the true strength of the nation lies in the strength of its people. The main purpose behind this book, as I've stated, is strengthening the level of morale we have in this country. I love my country and I have a great deal of faith in it and it's people, but one thing I've learned along this crazy seventeen-year journey called my life, is that before you can build or rebuild morale for something you believe in, you have to first check the confidence and principles you hold in yourself. And, America, we have lost that confidence over the last ten years. One of the first steps in repairing any issue we face is reconstructing our high confidence. The true strength of a nation lies in its people. In its individual.

I'm no "expert" on the subject, but I've been on this earth for seventeen years and I've given in to and done a lot of stupid things already. I've had my heart broken several times, I've been selfish, said stupid things, looked at things that would even embarrass Al Gore, disregarded my parents' authority, took out anger on the people I love, the list goes on and on. I've been, at times, a person that even I wouldn't want to be around. I'm no better than anyone else; in fact I'm probably worse than a lot. But I'm not a bad person. Neither is anyone else who has done stupid things. The real truth is that there are no bad people, just people who allow their mistakes and heartache to control them, instead of taking away from it, and learning.

I'm not going to sit here and claim to be perfect because I'm the farthest thing from it. If not for God's grace, mercy, and compassion, I would consider myself trash with every mistake I've already made. I'm just a person who chooses to do something with what little past he already has instead of trying to hide it. Someone who chooses to use his past, as a testimony. To quote the president, what I am here to do is to be as transparent as possible. It's a choice we all have to make. It's the mindset you choose to have when it comes to the mistakes and follies in your lifetime.

I believe that maybe, just maybe, people can learn from MY past or anyone else's for that matter. There is always more to learn, especially for me. I've learned things from realizing that I don't have all the answers. The answers lie in history and in the history of the heroes God has been gracious enough to put in my path. Even though its hard to believe sometimes, God must really love me. He gives me the opportunity, not only to learn from my own mistakes, but to learn from the past of those before me who love me enough to sew principle into my life. A past is something we all have in common. It holds our good times, our great times, our bad, our shining moments and closet skeletons. It's a part of our spirit that we will never be able to get rid of. Our past is emblazoned in the root of our hearts and memories for a reason.

God didn't accidentally make us that way. He put it there so that we could use it to our advantage. He didn't put it there so that we remember how bad we used to be. That's the last thing He intended for us. He put it in us in order to protect the plan and product He created us for; what He created us to be. He's put something special inside all of us, and has a plan even when it seems like our lives are spinning out of control.

In difficult periods of our life, we like to give in to pain, because we may feel unloved, alone, or isolated from the rest of the world. We don't want to believe that God is there.

God has been called a lot of things; Father, King, El Shaddai, Lord of lords, Redeemer, and friend. But one name for God that I've lately thought most of is "the Potter." The job of a potter is to transform a worthless lump of clay into something beautiful and worthy. When beginning a new project, the potter takes a nice fresh lump of clay and sets it on his turn table. He sets his foot onto the peddle and begins to spin the table, using his hands to mold the clay into the image he chooses. When the clay begins to harden, he wets down that hardened area. The clay is us. The bible refers to us as "clay, marred in the hands of the Potter."

He already knows what He's created us to look like

and act like and feel. We just have to trust that He has it all under control. He knows exactly what he's doing and even though He's proven that over and over again, sometimes the difficulty we face hardens our hearts. We begin to question ourselves, what we believe in, even who we are as people. We start turning away from God and ourselves, shutting out any sense of confidence or morality in our hearts. When we turn from him, we lose sense of what real happiness is. I've lived this. I've had to take a couple of emotional and mental beatings because of veering off the right path. I've been the person who loses sense of who he really is and I became something I wasn't because of it: A conformist and a quitter. I stopped fighting the wrong words and the wrong actions and started giving in to what I knew wasn't right. I gave in, I learned, and I'm a better person today because of it, and I still have learning to do. Better doesn't mean perfect, it means progress. We turn away at times and that's when God wets our hearts down with a lesson. Here's another moral question we deal with a lot: If God loves me so much, why do I go through all the crap I do? Why does He allow me to be put through so much? Answer this question for yourself: Two men are walking down a sidewalk. One of them is dressed in a suit, pockets bulging from his wallet, an expensive watch on his wrist, designer sunglasses covering his eyes, and the newest iPhone to his ear chatting it up. The other man is dressed in a ratty coat, shoes with holes in each sole, and smells like he just showered in a toxic waste dump.

A mugger jumps in front of the two men and holds them at gunpoint. Who do you think the mugger is more likely to rob? The man who looks like he has something worth stealing, or the one who doesn't? God allows us to be put through trials because He wants to protect what He's put inside of us. He knows the calling for greatness on each of our lives and He knows that the enemy wants to destroy that. He wants to ensure that when the enemy attacks, we are ready for him. We face hard times because the enemy knows that if he doesn't knock us down, or destroy what we are at the moment; God has something in store for us that will make us better than anything the world could throw at us. Yes it's hard, but we come out better people because of all the pride we've had to swallow. Trust me, I know it's hard to face pain, sometimes...or A LOT of the time. In fact, there have been points in my life when I've felt so defeated by it that my heart had become so hardened, my loved ones had no more desire to be around me or try to help.

For me, and the way it used to be, every time that I decided to open up to someone, it was to someone who didn't have my best interests at heart and I would end up getting hurt for it. Which in turn, caused me to lash out at the ones around me who actually did have my best interests at heart. I was raised and taught the ethics that I always found to be second nature: Always respect those in authority, tell the truth even when it might get you in trouble, use your words wisely, know what your talking about, don't talk bad about people behind their backs, stay awake in church, say your prayers, never quit, do what the Bible says, stay away from bad influences, don't let your temper get the best of you, always treat girls with dignity and respect, and be a good big brother to your siblings, etc. All of these are things my parents and mentors have been instilling in me since I've been old enough to learn, and I've always believed in and done my best to live by them.

But, eventually, society taught me that many people don't find these in a second nature concept. I have gone through periods in my life where holding true to principles was no longer supported, accepted and even found strange to some people. Standing up to a society that wages war on principle and ethics isn't exactly an easy thing to do, especially when you're a hormonal seventeen year old kid. But it's a war I've been fighting all my life and I've definitely lost plenty of battles in the war when it comes to making the right choices. What I had to learn was that the only person responsible for those choices and the consequences of making them was me. Sometimes, when you have people coming in and out of your life that don't accomplish anything but harm, even if its unintentional, it takes a serious toll on your heart.

One thing that took me a while to learn is that blaming others for your actions doesn't do anything to help you. It only hurts. You begin to lose sight of yourself. You start living to impress others and you start forgetting the support of the ones around you that you love. You begin to take it for granted. You start living your life in limbo where you don't go anywhere because you are too busy sitting around blaming God and the world for the mess they made of your life. As I've said before, your life is a chain reaction; a vicious cycle, if you will. God knows what He created you to be. If you surrender to Him and live a life of integrity the way He want us to, it doesn't mean you'll never face adversity, but it means that you'll be a better person because of the way you faced it.

But if you choose to go your own way and believe that God and the world are against you, though heartbroken, God will let you do so. But, from experience I can tell you, that will only bring you more and more heartache than anything. What people need to understand is that we are not just clay in the Potter's hands, we are marred, blemished and imperfect, but we are IN THE POTTER'S HANDS. No matter how far you run, God still has you. He loves you and

He'll never leave no matter how hard, fast, or long you run. He'll stay out of your business, but He'll never leave. If you get tired of the spinning table, just remember Whose foot is controlling the spinning. Remember, the Bible tells us that He'll never give us more than we can bear as long as He is involved in our lives.

An old friend of mine, a little while ago, lost her dad. Her parents were divorced before then and each had found new love interests. She was between houses a lot, and had plenty of trouble with teenage guys who don't understand how to treat a girl. I lost contact with her for a little while, but when she came back, she was totally different from when I had last spoken to her. She no longer trusted anyone, including me, her family, or even God.

She had let pain get the best of her. She fell into the wrong crowd and started doing things she knew weren't who she was. I have never lost a parent. I've faced divorce in my family, but never my own parents' divorce. I can only imagine going through all that she did and if anyone else judges her for falling, they're wrong to do so. I'm not calling her out, because I don't blame her for losing touch with God. I've seen people a lot stronger than her fall for smaller things. My point of this story is for you to understand that though we don't blame those who break down when they have every right to, we also don't remember them. We remember those who faced it head on and stood strong, even while the walls around them came down.

My friend had decided that she was content in the place where she had fallen. That trusting people who loved her wasn't worth the risk of getting hurt. She is no longer looking for real love, or happiness, but I pray that even though its not one of her priorities anymore, she will find them anyway. But this is happening to people all over. Part of the reason that we have struggled in society, is because we let society control us. Society is a structured community of PEOPLE. Not of robots, or animals, or puppets but people who have the ability to choose between decent and indecent.

Our lives don't control us. We have the power to be people who live by good decisions and overcome dark times, but we have to choose to stand for good and peaceful means. Even when the system is behaving wrongly or getting too big for its overpriced, corduroy pants, stand peacefully and respectfully in the way you know is right, and fight that way. Not with unruly disruptive sit-ins ... yes UNIONS I'm talking to you. Violence, attacks and vitriol will get you nowhere. We will always struggle with everyday life. Things are going to come our way that are hard to avoid or control, but what we can always control is the way we handle it and the person we allow it to make us. I'm no one special and I'm most certainly not better than anyone else. I've met many people who aren't as blessed to have had role models like mine and have come to be some of the best human beings I have ever had the good fortune of knowing. I have also met those whose parents were just as good as mine and have turned out to be people who chose a wrong path.

I'm no better than anyone else. I'm just a young American who loves his country enough to stand up for good against ignorance, against violence, and for the resurrection of morality and truthfulness in his country. It's the righteous indignation we find that pushes us to make a difference, whatever that difference may be. Writing this book was mine, maybe yours is a rally, a blog, a town hall meeting, or even a Facebook group. Whatever it is, don't burn out or ignore the fire in your gut. Speak up for what you believe, take it, and use it to make a difference; peacefully, strategically, and truthfully.

Have you ever heard the story about the man who prayed and asked God every day to win the lottery? He prayed and prayed every day that he would hit the jackpot, and went to church every Sunday. Finally God answered him and said, "buy a ticket." If there is something that you aspire to, don't just sit and expect it to happen for you. We don't sit by faith, we WALK by faith. Chase your blessings, and stand by your principles and values, because in the strength and standing of America's people, lies the strength of America herself.

Don't just hold tightly to principles when it comes to your opinions and political standpoints, but be a person of peace and virtue in your everyday life. Live by your values once you find them, and find a righteous indignation against injustice, and corruption. You have the power to be a person you know would make your forefathers proud. Don't give in to the pain or let-downs in your life. Remember it, learn from it, but don't revel in it. Not everyone will agree with you, and that's OK. That's a good thing. YOU just present YOUR stance and stand by it with honor, and be willing to hear theirs with an open mind and heart.

Know that even though people will hurt you, in the long run the only person responsible for the way your life turns out is you. Once you learn that, make the choice to learn from your pain and mistakes. Be a person of integrity, respect, and responsibility, and I promise, you will go far. I know it. I've lived it. This is one thing you can take my word on. You are strong, you can think, and no matter what anyone tells you, you are a good person. You just have to find faith, and courage in your heart, and hold on to it.

10

Love, Loss, And The Maturity Game

"I knew your mom was the one, because when I met her, I had lost everything. I was no knight on a white horse; it was more like I was walking behind my horse with a shovel. But she stayed anyway."
-Joseph Kenneth Clagett

Love hurts. Isn't that just the understatement of the year? What would I know about that anyway, right? I'm seventeen. Well, with the past few years of experience that I've gained on this subject, I've come to know more and more each day. I've been on the relationship roller coaster ride from hell and let's just say that in the course of the past two years of my life, I've established a pretty good perspective on the game, at least from a high school standpoint. And, since this is a "teen's perspective," that's exactly what you're gonna get. I'm not going to sit here and tell you that I know everything about this subject and that if you follow every detail of what I'm about to tell you, then everything is going to work out perfectly, because that just isn't how it is. Perfect is an interesting word to use when it comes to this topic. The truth is that there is no perfection. There is only each and every individual's versions of perfect. I wont say that this is exactly for you, but what I will say is that this is what I have learned fighting my own battles with love, and my hope is that maybe it can help someone else understand the game a little bit better.

Today, the majority of problems that tail along with relationship and romance in society, believe it or not, greatly resemble the issues of our country. Crazy thing to say? Maybe, but I'm going to try and explain why I've come to that conclusion. While you won't hear any major broadcasting companies running stories about this topic and its "conspiratorial, evil stranglehold" on society, it is a large portion of what makes the world, the world. Any relationship that a person enters into has the ability to control their mood, their day, their mindset and possibly any other relations they may have in the present or even the future.

As for me, and MY experiences in this subject, I've come to learn plenty. Nowhere near everything, and even further from enough, compared to most people, but I have learned a lot. A lot more than I claimed to know, say a few years ago when in all reality I had no idea what I was doing. While learning from mistakes can hurt, sometimes it's exactly what we need to get us to the point where God can really bless us. No one knows this statement to be truer than I do. You could say that I'm the type who wears his heart on his sleeve a little more than he should. Those who know me would agree with this statement in a heartbeat. Though sometimes I wish my lifestyle was different, God made me that way for a reason. Living that way has brought me pain, but in bringing me pain, it has brought me to some serious realization.

In fact, when this book was just a thought in my head, it was simply an aspiration at first. What pushed me over the edge from aspiration, to determination was heartbreak. Outside, in the winter weather of November, three miles from any transportation, on my knees in the middle of the road, tears freezing on my face, I could've given it all up. I could have become the next statistic just because some indecisive teenage girl that I had given too much away to, decided to walk out of my life.

Instead, through all the thoughts clouding my mind, and the blood pouring from my heart, I felt a passion inside me growing. I remembered the wise words of love from my family, my friends, and my pastor. At that moment, I knew I wasn't meant to be where I was. I had strayed from God's side, and He was calling me home. Walking back five miles toward the car, I whispered a prayer the whole way. That God would take my heart, and put His wisdom in my mind so that I could find the ability to follow His calling and write the book you now hold in your hands. I was done with allowing people to hurt me, but it wasn't the vengeful kind of done. It was a thankful kind. Thankful that even though I had been on one huge painful roller coaster ride, I had learned from it. It was no longer my killer, it became my testimony.

Now, maybe you're thinking that this story sounds a bit exaggerated, and you would be absolutely right. Looking back now, it's embarrassing to have been broken so immensely over something as minute as a teen relationship gone bad. But, that's just the kind of pain that God has made me to learn from. We all have different things to learn, and with those come struggle so that we CAN learn. I have always had problems when it came to relationships; much like most teenagers today. Relationships for anyone under the age of 25, are always a vicious cycle that follows the characteristics of each gender. Teenagers give in too easily to their pre-determined title in society today, where all younger guys are sex-driven jerks who only have one thing on their mind, and girls are supposed to be interested in that. That's supposed to just be the way it works. Well, if you're someone who finds that cycle ridiculous and immoral, and you choose to treat the opposite sex with respect, talk to them like they're human, and save yourself sexually until you're wedding day, you don't usually fit too well in this cycle. I used to choose to blind myself to this fact and to the signs one usually should see in the beginning, even though they were warnings that pretty much blared a "GET OUT NOW," siren.

Society today has been broken over this issue. When it comes to a relationship, people no longer know what to look for in another human being. I've been told since I was little, that there are no shortcuts in life, and I've come to realize that to be truer over the years. Not only are there no shortcuts in success, there aren't any shortcuts in anything worth finding. Not the answers to healing the nation, and not choosing your life partner. People today are deciding more often than not, that waiting around for the right person isn't all its cracked up to be. They choose to settle for the first thing that comes their way and only appears to have an answer.

They settle for the wolf-in-sheep's-clothing solution which actually does more harm to them, than good in the end. Isn't it weird how that sounds like exactly what we're doing to our country? Settling for the first and easiest thing that comes along claiming to have the answer? It's funny when you look at it how all issues in society connect themselves in one way or another. That is why I keep saying that the answer doesn't lie with higher-ups, it lies with the passion and drive of its people.

We as a people have to decide to stop settling for the "easy-out," and realize that anything worth fighting for comes with hardship and must be fought for with dedication. A much too rapidly growing generational curse over our society is divorce. Families are being broken and torn apart solely because someone who made a commitment wakes up one morning and decides they no longer feel the same way. I understand that the option of divorce is there for a reason and, in extenuating circumstances, I'd understand a little better, but these numbers today are RIDICULOUS, and do not lie.

To say "I do" used to mean something. Today, statistics show that forty one percent of all first marriages end in divorce. After that, if you get married again, the likelihood of the second marriage ending jacks up to sixty percent (1). I have family members that have had to face divorce. Thanks to a lapse in judgment, the entire family suffered because of it, especially members closely connected.

The biggest problem with relationships is that a large amount of the population has lost the ability to be alone or to know what they are looking for. We no longer know what to fall in love with. We feel like we have to have somebody there, or there's something wrong with us and we no longer care how or who that person is. We feel like unless we have someone there telling us they love us, we're inadequate. It breaks my heart to see what so many people, young and old, will endure just to have someone around to say "I love you."

Another thing I've learned is that once you finally learn

from your past failures, that is when God really delivers. Now, I am fully aware of how hard it is to actually LEARN from heartbreak, but when you do, happiness comes so much easier. Sometimes, you have to learn the same lesson over and over and OVER again. Each one more and more painful. I went through such a long painful rut that eventually I became numb to the reality of who I needed to be searching for in a relationship. I was settling and taking what I could get, and all it did was hurt me more and more each time. When I was growing up, I was blessed enough to be raised around Godly couples who taught me how to treat the person I'm with, the right way. What I WASN'T blessed with, however, was the ability to always see what's good for me, what I need and what I don't. That one I had to figure out on my own.

And Sweet Father in heaven, did I EVER figure it out! But, before I figured it out, I had to get hurt. I had to get a "bad Sky" on the top of my hands quite a few times before I finally got the message, "Hey genius, maybe you should stop settling for girls who you know probably aren't good for you." Yes, I have been hurt A LOT, but now I know exactly what I DON'T want in a person. I also can see the Christmas-lit warning signs coming from a mile away. As much as getting hurt … well, hurts, the failures are how we learn, how we adapt to the game. Yes, the relationship world is one big game. Once you learn how to play, everything gets a lot easier. Bad news is that the rules may change with age, but the game never ends. Not even in marriage as most married couples have told me (It just gets a lot less fun, so I've been told).

I never fit well in the cycle. Since November of my freshman year of High school, I've fallen down and picked myself up in a rut that I thought would never end. I had been through person after person who didn't know how to have a real relationship. I kept wondering what was wrong with me. I began to wonder why I couldn't hold on to someone for longer than an average of a couple of months. A good friend of mine spoke to me about it, and gave me some of the few words I had heard at this point in my life that actually made me want to keep looking.

She told me that my problem wasn't me, it was my taste. My problem was that I was giving my heart away so fast, and so fluently, that I didn't realize who I was putting myself up with. I had ideologically put on a pair of what I like to call "desert goggles." Meaning that after you've been stuck in a desert for so long, eventually anything you find begins to look appealing, even baggage. The reason I couldn't hold close to anyone is because they weren't the ones God wanted me with, they were just my warped desperate versions of decent. If there's anything I know about my heavenly Father, its that if it isn't His will for you to be somewhere, He'll step out and let you try it on your own because He knows as well as we do that we can't do these things without Him.

I was settling for less than what He intended for me. I'm not saying I was a better person than the girls I was settling with (well MOST of them anyway), I'm saying that they weren't whom God intended for me. I was going through so much heartbreak because I needed to learn the fundamental rules in choosing a partner: Commitment and enlightenment. I had to figure out what I needed, what I was searching for and how to let God take the reigns of the search. I was blaming every girl that walked in and out of my life for all the pain they had caused me when in actuality, the only one costing me hurt was me. When I finally began thanking them for the lessons I had learned and finally stopped lessening myself to what I had been, I found that happiness was a lot easier to find.

No more lies, no more indecisiveness, no more rut. Don't get me wrong, there will still be problems in the future, I'm sure. No relationship is perfect, and there is no planned-out fairytale ending. But, we find our own path and the one thing that I'm sure of is that as long as I remain faithful to God and hold true to myself, the path that I am walking is my version of perfect.

There isn't a secret. Just be patient, and stop settling for less. Don't conform to the viscous cycle of relationships today. Stand for your beliefs and aspirations and more importantly for yourself. Here's a secret: The more dignity you have, the more likely they are to come back. I've had girls come back after years of no contact, strangely enough, right around the time I find happiness again. Isn't that weird? When people walk out of your life, let them go. That just means that they weren't meant to be there. Sure, it is going to hurt and its okay to sit around and cry about it for a little bit. But don't linger. Get up and go be who you are. They'll realize what they had pretty quickly, but by the time they do, you'll be long gone. I know its hard. Sometimes you feel that crying over it makes it hurt less. But doing that for too long hinders you from living the great life you have ahead of you.

The answer to this problem is you. Girls, you are so much better than abuse; verbal, physical, or sexual. You are strong and beautiful no matter what any guy tells you. Be women who know what they want, and be smart about how you get it. Don't put up with someone who doesn't treat you the way God made you to be treated, I don't care how great you think he is. If he's one way when people are around and another when your alone, and you like him better during the first one, get rid of him, because he's not worth your time.

Guys, be men of respect. Be with someone because

you love them, not because of what you can get out of it. Don't focus your entire life around one girl because there is much more going for you than just your next relationship. If you enter into a relationship, avoid transforming it into a dictatorship. Control of one person over the other should never be a factor, whether it is you controlling her or the other way around. There are ways to make her as happy as she makes you without turning yourself into a human doormat, and girls that goes for you, too. Know the boundaries and know the fine line between partnership and dictatorship. Then, know how they deserve to be treated and treat them even better than that.

Know what it is that you search for in a person, and align your own rules and boundaries.

SKY'S TOP 3 ADVANCE WARNING SIGNS AND RULES

1: If she doesn't know what she wants after a couple of months, run.

2: If her phone, often times "doesn't work," run.

3: If she's five feet or less and Italian, I PROMISE that's a bad mixture. Run.

When you know what you're searching for, it makes it a lot easier to find. Set goals and align boundaries and things become a lot easier. Not every relationship is going to be like the previous. So don't base them on your past. If you do that, you're only predetermining your own future and screwing any good thing that may be in it. When you enter into a relationship, as all successful couples will tell you,

you give up the "ME" for "US." Whatever hurts you hurts the other. Whatever makes you happy should make them happy. It's a partnership and you can't have that if only one person is willing to commit. Realize that communication is key. If there's a problem, don't just pretend it's not there because that will kill you. Talk about things and work them out together like a partnership is meant to work. Know how to hold on the right way. Not with jealousy, or distrust, but with love.

Why waste away what took you so long to find? Show them every day how important they are to you. It doesn't always have to be some big blowout Valentines Day sentiment, but give just a little more each day. When you are in a relationship, you are WITH someone. That means that there will be times when you have to sacrifice, emotionally or otherwise. Rough times will come, make no mistake, but the important thing is that you lay down at night knowing you'll wake up the next morning by the perfection that will be yours someday - if it isn't already. You can find your version of perfect, even in this crazy game. You just have to perfect "you" first.

11
Same America, New Generation

"Raising children is an incredibly hard and risky business in which no cumulative wisdom is gained: each generation repeats the mistakes the previous one made."
-Bill Cosby

I was the in-church texter. I was the kid that was constantly getting yelled at for having his phone out while the pastor was preaching. Way back when, I didn't understand the whole "shut up and listen" concept. When things started being said on stage, that I couldn't understand, my two-inch attention span would break and I would look for anything to keep myself pre-occupied and from having to pay attention to the front (yes, a lot of the time that even meant sleeping).

It wasn't because I meant to show disrespect to

God or the pastor. I just didn't understand then that a relationship with God or with anyone else has to grow through enlightening yourself in His word. Back then, when I didn't understand some of the things being said, I would shut out new experiences and new information. I was one who thought research and self education was a waste of my "valuable time," which usually consisted of video-games, nickelodeon, and oversized portions of Frosted Flakes. I didn't bother to look into what was being said, or trying to understand it. One thing that I've always heard growing up in church that really used to throw me off is when a speaker starts talking about the "burden they had for the upcoming generation."

I have a friend who is the son of a pastor. He's always been up for preaching publicly, and has always done it with passion, and a drive that most people his age don't have. He has always presented himself with pride and compassion for others, and has made it to a point in his life which garners my deepest respect toward him. He once preached a sermon back in 2007, which focused a lot on "this generation," and what was wrong with it. I watched him tear up when he spoke about his "generational burden." How he hurts to see teenagers going where they are today when they have so much going for them if they'd just "open up to the plan God has."

Well, needless to say, I was jealous. My mindset was not that I necessarily longed for his burden, but that I wanted to be as good a person as he was. A generational burden sounded like something that I should have, but for some reason, I just didn't. I had a sense of empathy, but I couldn't find a yearning in my heart for the pain of anyone else. I didn't know how to have one, or why I needed one. All I knew was I couldn't find it in me to care about the rest of the teenage population, when I had too many problems to deal with myself. But I wanted to, so I started trying to see through my pastor friend's eyes. Long story short, it didn't work. I remained apathetic to the problems he saw, and resentful because they weren't my own.

Eventually, I just gave up. I figured it was better to just not care the way I did, than to pretend to care as much as someone else does. So one day, I was at my grandparents' house getting some work done, and if your grandparents are anything like mine, the news channel is on their TV perpetually. I saw what was on the television, as the newscaster spoke about where the country was going. He spoke about the problems and the massive downturns that were raising the level of survival mode to critical, and what the people in power were doing and saying that they thought would "fix the problems."

It scared me to see so many power-hungry higher-ups lacking common sense. It scared me to see the filth and garbage that was polluting the minds and hearts of MY own people. It made me fear for the future of my country and my friends. It was in that moment that the question crossed my mind: "What about my generation? Is this going to affect us too? What about all the teenagers who don't know or care about what's going on? Or the ones who have bought into the lies and corrupted mindset of today's society? What's gonna happen when the real world hits us?"

Questions and fears pounded my brain in a matter of minutes. My heart was heavy as I thought about the possibility of the death of our nation. I fell back in my chair and realized that I had found the burden of my generation I was searching for and it was in the fear of its future. It wasn't that I couldn't care. It was that I hadn't yet found what to care about. I had to look in the right places, which aren't necessarily the places someone else has already found. My pastor friend found his generational burden through how teenagers were affecting their future by their own choices. I found mine through how our future is being affected by the actions of today's politicians and the corroded view of America that was, AND IS, being shoved down the throats of my people on a daily basis. Let me ask you some questions: Was the Pledge of Allegiance "controversial" when you were in school? Were you taught that your future is pretty much already gone thanks to the "evil," out-of-date Constitution? Were you taught that the old way of America, founded in 1776 on hard work, patriotism, and respect, needs to be changed because it just doesn't work and never will? AND was teaching communism, Marxism, progressivism, or socialism even an option?

Un-American ideology and youth indoctrination has infiltrated and infested our schools and our own homes in an attempt by the Progressives and Marxists of today to raise our children in a way that they see fit. What THEY see fit is a transformation of old American ideals like hard work, free speech and honor to ideals of political correctness, violence and pretty much any other socialistic virtue they can pull out of their bag of tricks. In April of 2011, the ACLU, who jumps on any opportunity to stamp out American culture, sent a letter to administrators of the Sweeny Independent School District in Texas claiming that the district's requirement of students having to stand during the pledge of Allegiance tramples the first amendment of the students and that their policy needed to be changed no later than April 21. Disturbingly, the ACLU won and the policy was changed at the wish of two students, one of which stated, *"I personally do not wish to stand and I shouldn't be forced to do so."* As all **COWARDS** go out, the ACLU did not name either student at their request to remain anonymous. (I'm their age and I will brand them how I wish, and by the way, my name is **SKY KENNETH CLAGETT**). Now, not only are the pledge's words becoming controversial, but showing respect for it is as well. In Brookline Massachusetts, Principal Gerardo Martinez of a public school called The Devotion School, sent out permission forms to the parents of students in order to allow the students to take part in reciting the pledge every week.

In March of 2011, a few teachers of LA and New York gathered together to discuss how to use their connections as teachers to push Marxism and social justice in the classroom. Oh yeah, did I mention that these teachers were involved in Unions? One teacher, Sarah Knopp, who donned a "Tax the Rich" T-shirt claimed that the best way to *"empower your students"* is to be *"Involved in struggles for economic justice and to change the economic priorities of this [current] system and to change the economic system as a whole."*

Not only are our kids being indoctrinated by Marxists and socialists, but by ex-felons. An article in the New York Post confronted the issue of parental outrage due to felons teaching in public schools of New York City. Mayor Bloomberg claimed that there was nothing he could do about it: *"There are very strict rules in the existing contract that prohibit the city from deciding in this case whether these people should be in the classroom."* Where is the person who will stand up and say, "Screw the contract. This is our youth." That person needs to be found and fast. My generation is slowly being torn apart by indoctrination.

Most teens today HATE politics, which is understandable. I hate politics. But, what I realize is that the more that you are aware of, the easier it is to keep on a right course. While some are aware, many of my generation have either chosen a path of vitriol instead of peace, or have shut out anything about what's going on in the world right now. Today, we are turning everything into a fantasy world. Cell phones (put me on that list), iPods (put me at the top of that list), teenage relationships (I AM that list), and any other current thing that we can get a hold of is automatically used to shut out the real world.

In 2008, Mr. Barack Obama reached out to the younger generation, and instantly became a rock star. Mr. Obama's campaign cronies spent countless hours and dollars on a hostile takeover of teens via their own domain: Cell phones, iPods, music, television and the internet. Yes, Facebook too. Co-creator of Facebook, Mr. Chris Hughes - and Mr. Joe Rospars of Blue State Digital were responsible for creating for Mr. Obama his own social networking website called "**my.barackobama.com**," recently updated as "**barackobama.com**." Cronies even had their own sex-angle, which they took full advantage of in 2007 through Mr. Obama's own "*Obama girl*," Amber Lee Ettinger who debuted in her own half-naked, scandalous music video on youtube.com called "***Crush on Obama***." The whole nation had been shifted into a state of unhealthy idolization, and Mr. Obama went down in history as one of the most expensive campaigners ever. Even Apple Inc. and Google pitched in to help fund Mr. Obama's campaign. "Well of course, because Mr. Obama is so influential and clearly the better candidate, having written two books on himself and gone to law school. Big corporations just can't help but to want to pitch in." Well, not so much. Apple and Google just so happen to share a similar factor: Al Gore, the famous environmental money-hungry alarmist, who loves public appearances, summertime scare tactics, and masseuse girls. AND who just happens to be a member of the directing board at Apple, and a senior adviser at Google. Man, he must have a great lonely old-guy online dating profile. Colleges, high schools, and ignorant, mind numbing television stations (*cough*cough MTV) had all been obamafied and were spreading it across the nation like a cancer.

Today's younger voters were pushed to ignore any red flag that came along with Mr. Obama. Any remaining sense of reality in the election was sucked dry. "Wait, President Obama is friends with Bill Ayers, a sick twisted 70's activist bomber? And, his racist pastor, Jeremiah Wright, who is friends with Islamic extremists, claims in his own words to hate America, and has run Mr. Obama's self proclaimed home-church for the last twenty years by the rules of Marxism, socialism, and black supremacy with death to 'rich folk'? AND, in his seven years in office as a senator of Illinois, instead of voting for or against a bill, he voted 'present' 129 times and his only accomplishment was writing two books about himself? Hmmm….Oh well, who cares about all that? After all, he's black!"

Ahhh yes….nothing like a little peace, sense, and "racial unity" to make an American presidential election. Teenagers and the younger generation of today are being brainwashed of what little sense remains after puberty hits. They are also being heavily affected by the actions and decisions being implemented in Washington. Using the destructive ideals of political correctness and progressivism, my generation is being crippled. Because of this, there is a massive generational gap in America. Teenagers no longer have the proper guidance and have been left to the leadership of those on a wrong path and pre-made labels; labels that have been pinned to teenage populations for a long time. Labels that include the idea that all we are about is drugs, sex, and the weekend. Ideas that our feelings shouldn't be hurt by red pens, or that differing opinions shouldn't be allowed, are all examples of things that are destroying us.

What makes these labels ten times worse is that today, our guidance is left in the hands of what we see six slow, uneducated ding-dongs doing on ***Jersey Shore***. We conform to the labels around us and we're being indoctrinated and raised by the conforming ideals of current society. If you don't think government affects you as a teenager, you're dead wrong. Remember all the ideals set forth by progressives I talked about earlier? How we aren't smart enough to think for ourselves, learn from failure, or control our emotions? The whole red pen thing? School indoctrination? Marxism? Political correctness? It all applies to us. Government today is sealing this generation away from reality because "It's just too scary. We need to protect our children from all those big bad scary things out there." Newsflash: scary things are out there in the real world. If you're too busy trying to wimpify us or distort American principle, rather than teaching us how to live our lives properly and successfully in the perfect nation founded in 1776, then when we get out there, the real world is gonna hit and hit hard. My generation's current wimpification and desensitization, mixed with a lack of real guidance, plays as a deadly toxin for our future and it scares me to see what will happen when we get there and it 's in our hands.

Today's teenage generation, I believe, is the inheriting generation. Before the hippie era of the 60's and 70's, grandparents, and great grandparents worked hard to see that the generation of the 60's and 70's would inherit a country that they would be proud to live in. But what did youth do with that society when they received it? They began a movement of drugs, sex, hatred, ignorance, and violence, destroying everything those before them achieved. They made the hard work of their loved ones before them to be in vain. Now, what's crazy is that today's generation is being pushed to rise up the same way, not by radical government haters, but by the government itself infested from the inside by the same radicals! Today, we are given the same choice as back then, and we're blowing it all over again, except now, we are no longer as boldly open about it as the youth back then. My prayer is that we are able to change this course before it destroys us, because I know it's possible for us to do so.

Teenagers today are also destroying their futures by conforming to today's decaying society. Fifteen percent of American EIGHTH graders have admitted to trying weed, and approximately fifteen percent of sophomores and seniors have used amphetamines. Twenty five percent of seizures reported in hospitals come from the use of these amphetamines, and 1.8 million teenagers today, age twelve and older are active users of cocaine. The National Institute of Justice has reported that sixty six percent of teenage male arrestees test positive for pot. Alcohol kills six and one-half times more teenagers than drug use, and underage drinking costs the U.S. itself more than $58 billion EVERY year. There are 820,000 girls under the age of twenty reported to have been pregnant each year and approximately one in FOUR teens are reported with some form of STD EACH YEAR. Thirteen percent of all U.S. teenagers have had vaginal sex by the age of fifteen and by age nineteen, seven in ten teens have engaged in sexual intercourse. According to **www.teendepression.org**, at least twenty percent of teens will also experience depression before they reach adulthood.

If you're under age twenty five, and you're reading this book, go ahead and read the above just a few more times. This is you. These numbers are our people, and our people are dying day by day from stupid decisions because we're not listening to the right voices. This is OUR story. Is this how we want to write it? Those statistics are just a few examples, there are plenty worse out there, but I'll leave that research to you. Why do we have to be the next drug addicts, or drunks, or next few statistics? Nowhere is that written. I believe in my generation, even if no one else does. Why? Because, I know PEOPLE, not statistics. I know teenagers who aren't conforming to these numbers, and won't give in to pre-made labels. They stand up against the grain, and people look up to them. I know teenagers who go through a whole lot more crap than a lot of adults that I know, and they come out still holding on strong. I know teenagers who, despite what their home life is like, how their daily lives go, or how much they hate their jobs, continue to work on themselves and try to become the shining light that they already are to me and everyone else around them.

These are the teenagers who should be the face of my generation. Not Lindsay Lohan or Paulie D., but regular every day teenagers who live their lives by not-so-everyday principles and integrity. Do you want to see what happens when generational gaps swallow society? Look at who our leadership and impressionability is being left to. We all know who Superman is, right? The iconic DC comic book hero that's been around since 1942 defending the innocent and fighting for "truth, justice, and the American way." Well, the latest issue to come out was the nine-hundredth issue entitled, "The Incident." In this issue, the Man of Steel says to the U.S. President, *"Truth, justice and the American way"- Its not enough anymore. I'm tired of having my actions construed as instruments of U.S. Policy."* Doesn't this sound a lot like the "America is bad," globalist trend that is being shoved down the throats of American youth today? Well, if you think so, don't worry. Jim Higgins of ***the Journal Sentinel*** puts all of us "narrow minded, over reactionary" Americans at ease: *"First off, the Superman story in question, "The Incident," is a 9-pager tucked in the nearly 100 pages of Action Comics #900. It isn't the lead story nor is it rewritten by regular Superman writers. "This will probably never again be referenced" by anyone at DC, and might not even be "in continuity" (meaning it's not likely to be part of the official timeline of Superman stories going forward).*

Mr. Higgins also turns to Ben Moore of ***Screen Rant*** who continues to "comfort" us with his infinite left-wing wisdom. He argues that Superman was just being dramatic. If writers really wanted to "renounce his citizenship," it would've been done in a bigger more serious way. *"It would've been its own storyline with every single major character (Batman, Flash, Green Lantern, Wonder Woman, Green Arrow, and so on) making an appearance to say something about, I don't know — America."* Oh well now, I feel so much better knowing that Superman was just throwing a hissy fit. Thank you Mr. Moore for clearing all that up for us. It doesn't matter how "unserious" the writers meant it to be. What matters is that my generation is seeing it. We are who this is meant for and we see it, whether ***Screen Rant*** or ***the Journal Sentinel*** believes that or not. This is serious because it ties into the control over my generation that indoctrinating socialists and Marxists of America (those words just should not ever go together) are fighting hard for.

There is a website called www.mariatalks.org that is meant to teach kids about Sex Education. I've gotta tell you, Georg Lukacs may as well have designed this website himself. This website was designed by the AIDS Action Committee (AAC) with help from the Massachusetts Department of Health. This is a site for teens to get information about sex, pregnancy or STD's. But, the information is indoctrination in sheep's clothing. On the subject of talking to a doctor, the site says, *"Sex is a private thing between you and your partner, but it is also a big part of your current and future health, just like eating right, not smoking, and exercising. So expect your doctor to ask you (in private, with your parents OUT of the room) about your sex life."* Absolutely! Sex is extremely private between two people. But we're talking about teenagers. This site, on more than one occasion, discourages teens from involving their parents with the decision of sex or pregnancy such as in contacting family planning agencies. *"All of your information will be strictly confidential and they will never tell anyone your business, not even your parents, unless you give them permission to do so (usually in writing). It's actually illegal for them to disclose your information without your permission, even to your parents, (I bet that comes as a relief). What's also cool is that if you want help to talk to your parents about your decision, they will totally help you with that too."*

Don't worry, Planned Parenthood organizations are legally bound to not disclose your personal information to anyone, not even those horrible parents of yours. Isn't that great? Oh wait, you actually want to tell them? Oh...well... they can do that too. Indoctrination comes in many forms. Some more great examples from this site:

- *"You should also know that someone under 18 can give consent for an adoption in Massachusetts. They don't need to get permission from a parent."*

- *"I also know that the information I share with her won't be shared with anyone else—including my parents."*

- *"If you are under 18 and have decided that abortion is right for you, you can call the Planned Parenthood Counseling and Referral Hotline at 1-800-***-****. They can either help you talk to your parents, or if you decide that you can't or don't want to do that, they will provide you with a free lawyer who will help you go to court and talk to a judge."*

One more thing on mariatalks.com. I just want you to read their words on abortion and adoption and tell me if you can feel the "nonbiased" care in their hearts:

> ADOPTION: *"Once you choose an adoption agency, the agency can then help you decide what type of adoption works best for you and your baby. From what I've heard, going through this process can be pretty tough for some people, especially emotionally. Agencies will provide resources and support for people who are having a rough time and will help them get through it. There is also support for anyone close to you who may also be affected by the decision."*

> ABORTION: *"Abortion is a pretty hot topic with some of the kids at my school. Some believe that it is wrong while others believe that it can be a good and responsible choice. While everyone is entitled to their opinion, it can sometimes be hard to get truthful information because some people may try to get you to think the same way they do. What's important is how you feel about it. One of my friends who had an abortion told me that it was a difficult decision to make, but she felt that it was the best choice she could make for herself, her boyfriend, her family, and her future."*

> *"Ok, I totally know that this information can sound pretty intimidating and overwhelming, but I promise you the reality of getting an abortion is much easier than it sounds here."*

> *"Again, I know it sounds crazy, but just keep reading . . . this really can be done and young women do this all the time here in Massachusetts."*

Ahhh yes ... you feel that loving, friendly nonpartisanship in the air? No, adoption is scary and bad. It's much better to trust financially-run jerks like Planned Parenthood who'll kill your baby for you. These are the voices that are leading our teens in the midst of this generational gap. Are these the voices that we want to entrust our future with? The ones that are trying to shove the ideas down our throats that America is bad the way it was founded, and things need to be changed violently and swiftly?

We have to present a united front that listens to the right voices or the future of this country is lost, because we are its future. We are the next beneficiaries, and its time to insure that what we're inheriting is the nation that America was made to be: A country founded on strength and morality. Not sex, drugs, violence, or the next high, but family, love, hard work and integrity. I believe that there can be a teenage rebellion unlike that of the 60's and 70's; a rebellion not against authority, but against the low expectations previously set forth for teenagers. Don't think that because you're young and have no voting right that you have no power in this nation. YOU are the next leaders, and its time to start acting like it. Its time for a movement. I'm looking for someone to stand up to say, "I'll lead."

Believe it or not, people today are searching desperately

for youth who love their country enough to stand up for it. I've stepped up, because I do love my country and I refuse to be silent any longer. I refuse to allow its future to be decided for me by people who openly hate what it stands for. I will fight, by the principles outlined in 1776 and this book by God and the founders of America, to the bitter end for my country and people. But I can't do this alone. Please don't leave ME to be the one who leads this movement, because I can't do it alone. I'm nowhere near perfect. That is why the movement can't be left to just one leader.

The leader has to be the whole pack. Don't expect one person to pull us all. Instead, let's all pull the country. If we band together, they will listen. They're searching for us. Don't act violent or stupid, but be enlightened, and know what you're talking about. Be someone who stands up for America's future, someone who stands up for common sense, abstinence, or for the life of an infant. Or someone who stands against the use of drugs, or someone who is a role model for the smaller kids. Find your voice because you have it somewhere in you and it's a whole lot stronger than you think. Don't get me wrong, cars and money sound pretty great to me too. The real challenge is, knowing how to achieve those dreams, if that's what your dreams include. We all have different hopes and aspirations, but we can all get them the same way: Through hard work, dedication, and a sense of honor and responsibility.

Guys, its time to be the role models you know you have the ability to be. Don't sleep around with girls just because you can. Heck, I've seen ugly guys do that. It takes a real man to say, "No, I'm saving myself." That's power. Any boy can smoke, pick fights, gamble or whore around, but it takes a man to have the power to say no to that crap. Girls, don't belittle yourselves to please anyone else, because you don't have to. Don't sleep around because it makes you feel good about yourself, because you're already God's most beautiful creation. He made Adam first, because he saved the best for last. Be strong, and independent.

I've been in school assemblies before and I know personally how hard it is to hear rants and not laugh them off. If you want to ignore what I'm saying, you go right ahead, but you just know that your future family and possibly even your present, will suffer for it greatly. You can't be the conformist. Stand up. It's time to close this generational gap. Those before us have great stories, and information to give us to prepare, so let's take advantage of it, while we still have a chance. Start listening to the right voices.

I can tell you right now, those voices aren't coming from the government and they wont be ANY time soon. To find the right voices, use your brain and your heart and hold tight to your dreams. Its okay to have them. Have faith and they may just become reality, no matter how "out there" they seem. Truth be told, one day, I'm gonna marry Bridgit Mendler (Its gonna happen, she just doesn't know it yet). Dreams may be crazy but they've proven themselves over and over. Even the craziest thing out there can become real. Unfortunately, I don't think my dream above applies to that. Its been said, "*Shoot for the moon. Even if you miss, you'll land among the stars.*" One of the best parts is that you don't have to get there on your own. Look to the grandparents, the parents, the regular working class, HONEST and honorable citizens of America for guidance. It's time for us to stand up, unite, and start a revolution. Not a violent revolution of yelling and screaming fits, banging on desks and exploding with curse words like a bunch of ACORN reps, but a revolution run by peace, principle, enlightenment, integrity, and honesty. A revolution that saves the future of our nation, and the future of the new generation.

12

America 2.0

"I pray Heaven to bestow the best of blessings on this house, and on all that hereafter inhabit it. May none but honest and wise men ever rule under this roof."
-John Adams, referring to White House

On October 31, 2008, President-elect Barack Hussein Obama said this: *"We are just five days away from fundamentally transforming the United States of America."* America was founded and established in 1776 by men who longed for nothing more than a fair shot at life, liberty, and the pursuit of happiness. Men, who believed in limited government and relied firmly on their faith in God's grace and strength, and in the morality and resiliency of the human spirit. America has been said to be the last best hope of the earth, because it is one of the only countries left founded on freedom, dreams, and individual happiness. So ask yourself, is it still worth saving? Or, are you willing to allow today's radicals to transform it into something totally different?

When you've lived in a house all your life, that you've fallen in love with, it inevitably begins to show its age and abrasion. At that point, what do you do with it? Do you tear it down, and build something totally different in its place, or do you restore it to its state of original beauty? This is a question we need to answer for ourselves in the context of our nation. If you love something, you don't want to change it, you want to restore it because to you, its value is worth restoring. America has fallen. It's showing serious wear and tear. We can't seem to fix our problems, people are going blind to who is in power anymore and we are losing sight of what this nation was originally built on. People are scared, and when people get scared, they will accept anyone who comes along claiming to have an answer.

Unfortunately, for the founders or anyone who still believes in principle and common sense, the only answer that most people in power can come up with today is transformation of America. The real question is, "Into what??" The scariest thing that I've ever seen is the American society that I am living in today. And what's even more scary, is that from what I've gathered, even when some people find out what the truth is, they openly accept it and become a part of it. In this final chapter, I'm going to blow your mind with some of the scariest truths you have ever heard.

The truth is that today, the president of the United States' entire frame of mind and moral conscience has been morphed and formed by people who openly wish to change the U.S. They are radicals and they are dangerous. President Obama has a dark past that many "raving fans" seem to be ignoring. Not only has Mr. Obama's entire life been lived through the ideals of radicalism, but to this day, he continues to voluntarily surround himself with people and groups who run their lives through un-American ideals of radicalism, socialism, Marxism, progressivism, population control, homosexual supremacy, globalism and out-of-hand, massive government control.

In February of 2007, when an Illinois senator announced his decision to run for the office of president, I took him in with an open mind. If you're like any other freedom loving American, you allow everyone that comes into the political game the fair chance to sway you in their direction. So when I start doing my research and I come to find out that Mr. Obama has been radically raised and surrounded by dangerous people for his entire life, maybe I'm crazy but for some odd reason that raises a serious red flag to me. What's even more crazy, is that the very, very, very, very, VERY few honest people that there are in the media who ARE reporting on his past, are being demonized NONSTOP and without mercy by other media networks and individuals, along with the rest of the "nonpartisan" political empire. By the end of this final three-part chapter, you will have a better understanding of "hope and change," and even more importantly, an easier decision to make.

PART ONE: The ~~Prodigal~~ Progressive Son

President Obama's connection to radicals isn't new and it didn't begin when he entered the political world. He has been subjected to their ideals and lifestyle since his own life began its course. Just look at who he considers his spiritual leaders. People like Saul Alinsky, social activist of the 70's who authored the book ***Rules for Radicals***. And what better way to kick off a radical organizer's rule book than an acknowledgement to Satan? That's right, in the first few pages of Alinksy's book he wrote an acknowledgement to whom he considers "the first radical":

"Lest we forget at least an over the shoulder acknowledgement to the very first radical: from all our legends, mythology, and history (and who is to know where mythology leaves off and history begins-or which is which). The first radical known to man who rebelled against the establishment and did it so effectively that he at least won his own kingdom-Lucifer."

Check it out for yourself. The back of the book even states how Mr. Alinsky has played the role of political inspiration to both Mr. Barack Obama and Ms. Hillary Clinton. Even from childhood, Mr. Obama and his family have lived by principles that weren't exactly "American," and it shows through the decisions that he makes as commander-in-chief. For the sake of avoiding argument, let's just go, for a second, with what the records say: Barack Hussein Obama, Jr. was born in Honolulu in 1961 to Stanley Ann Dunham who had been abandoned by the blood father named Barack Hussein Obama, Sr., a devout Muslim from Kenya (I know, that's a weird combo). Sadly, young Barack, Jr. was abandoned again by his stepfather, who was also Muslim, Lolo Soetoro. In 1967, Mr. Obama was enrolled in a Muslim school called Fransiskus Assisi in Indonesia under the Muslim name of Barry Soetoro.

In Hawaii, Obama, Jr. lived with his grandparents in Honolulu where he attended Punahou prep school from 1971 to '79. According to Mr. Obama himself, he learned much during his childhood from a man named Frank Marshall Davis - a columnist for the Communist Party USA's Hawaii newspaper the ***Honolulu Record***. He befriended young Barack's family after they'd migrated from Kansas to Honolulu, Hawaii. A little freakier: A report from the Commission of Subversive Activities in 1951 identified Mr. Marshall Davis as a long-standing public member of the Communist Party USA, who had been accused in his day of being largely involved in communist organizations and factions in America, by the HUAC (House of Un-American Activities Committee) - who you heard about in chapter seven. Mr. Obama speaks of "the old poet, Frank" in his book ***Dreams of my Father***, and quite a few times dubs Davis as one of his "mentors." He also reminisces on one of the conversations they shared just before young Barack headed for college:

*"He studied me over the top of his glasses. 'Understand something, boy. You're not going to college to get educated. You're going there to get trained. They'll train you to want what you don't need. They'll train you to manipulate words so they don't mean anything anymore. They'll train you to forget what it is that you already know. They'll train you so good, you'll start believing what they tell you about equal opportunity and the American way and all that s***. They'll give you a corner office and invite you to fancy dinners, and tell you you're a credit to your race. Until you want to actually start running things, and then they'll yank on your chain and let you know that you may be a well-paid, well-trained nigger, but you're a nigger just the same.' 'So what is it you're telling me–That I shouldn't be going to college?' Frank's shoulders slumped, and he fell back in his chair with a sigh. 'No. I didn't say that. You've got to go. I'm just telling you to keep your eyes open. Stay awake.'"*

Mr. Obama eventually enrolled in occidental college where it has been rumored that he registered under false pretenses as a foreign student from Indonesia in 1979 in order to gain financial aid. I will give President Obama the benefit of the doubt on this subject. But, I'm not completely ruling it out, as there are instances of Mr. Obama's past that would lead one to conclude that it is very possible. But I'll let you look into that yourself. Before finally getting his famous law degree from Harvard Law in 1991, Mr. Obama worked behind the scenes in his community as an organizer (which is politically correct for riot starter) in the windy city, Chicago. It was there that he began finding new connections with radical groups like the Democratic Socialists for America and Students for a Democratic Society (SDS).

In 1992, Mr. Obama became a professor of law at the University of Chicago Law. Between then and 2004, he ran for a senate seat in Illinois. During that time he also did legal work for *Project Vote*, an ACORN derivative. ACORN is the Association of Community Organizations for Reform Now. ACORN is the mother load of capitalist-hating American progressivism today. ACORN is notorious in the U.S. for multiple accounts of fraud and felony charges. In 2008, I'm sure you recall the voter fraud charge ACORN was pinned with for illegally registering deceased citizens, celebrities, and the lovable Disney characters as U.S. voters.

According to Robert Knight's ***Radical Rulers***, as an attorney Mr. Obama represented ACORN in a "Motor Voter" case in Illinois. Motor Voter is an invitation to voter fraud that allows one to register to vote using only a postcard and blocking the registering state from reducing voter rolls. 1,762 ACORN registrations were invalidated and seven ACORN workers were faced with felony charges, some of which already had previous criminal records. They are notorious for waging smear campaigns, and in some cases, violence against institutions or financial organizations that require eligibility for a citizen to qualify for a loan.

In 2009, ACORN advocates were caught on video giving advice to people about how to cheat on their tax forms and operate underage prostitution businesses under the radar of the federal government. A couple went undercover as a thirteen year old prostitute and her pimp seeking advice on how to run a prostitution business with underage girls from El Salvador. Two ACORN officials proceeded to give the 'couple' advice about how to cheat on their taxes by getting child tax credit for the underage El Salvador girls. They also fathered them on how to "*cover their a***" by making prostitution a "*legal business by using tax codes*" and "*teaching them [the El Salvador girls] to keep their mouths shut*," just in case they get in trouble with the law.

From childhood, Mr. Obama has found himself in webs of radical ideology and a wide array of Un-American felonious organizations. However, even as president of the United States, Mr. Obama continues to allow them into his inner circle. To say that these connections are accidental, or even more than a coincidence would be a major understatement. These connections are persistent and voluntary on Mr. Obama's part. Why is that? Because believe it or not, he shares many of the same ideals as those he surrounds himself with. B. H. Obama is the most controversial candidate that America has ever seen. From the beginning of his public and political existence, he has been leaving red flags all over the place. He has had a bipolar voting record, he has been surrounded with, and involved in, some of the most radical and violent organizations and people that the world has ever seen. We can't find many records on him, and what little we do find have come out in pieces. People instantly drew him in, because he came in running on the basis of change. But so far America, the only thing that this president has shown to change is his mind.

It's almost as if he doesn't believe in anything.

He says he doesn't condone or support water boarding because its torture. Yet he takes credit for the death of a major terrorist figure, Osama Bin Laden, when the information on Bin Laden's whereabouts comes from using the water boarding tactic. He comes in as president on the campaign promise to never use signing statements, which are presidential signings that overrule a congressional vote. UNTIL the legislation, or budget compromise, threatens to stop funding four of Mr. Obama's czars (whom you'll hear about in the next part of this chapter), then all of a sudden, when he's about to lose his beloved radical buddies, his words don't matter much. On the National Day of Prayer in 2009, Mr. Obama did not hold any White House event or national prayer as presidents in the past have done. But of course, on September 1, 2009, Mr. Obama held an Iftar banquet at the White house to honor the Muslim holy month of Ramadan. Wait, hasn't Mr. Obama claimed multiple times that he is a Christian? So, wouldn't the national day of prayer be kind of important to a devout Christian? Mr. Obama's home church was Trinity United Church of Christ for twenty years. That sounds legitimate to me. Oh wait! His pastor was a flamingly racist pundit named Jeremiah Wright who continually preaches capitalism and American hatred, black supremacy, and the downfall of that no-good, down-right evil, 'rich folk.' Some of Wright's preaching's include:

"Jesus was a poor black man who lived in a country and in a culture controlled by rich white people...We live in a culture that is controlled by and run by rich, white people. He taught me, Jesus did, how to love my enemies. Jesus taught me how to love the hell out of my enemies and not be reduced to their level of hatred, bigotry, and small-mindedness."

"Barack knows what it means, living in a country and

a culture that is controlled by rich white people. Hillary can never know that. Hillary ain't never been called a nigger!"

And of course, Wright's famous speech on the Sunday after September 11, 2009:

"We bombed Hiroshima, we bombed Nagasaki, and we nuked far more than the thousands in New York and the Pentagon, and we never batted an eye. We have supported state terrorism against the Palestinians and black South Africans, and now we are indignant because the stuff we have done overseas is now brought right back to our own front yards. America's chickens are coming home to roost."

"The government gives them the drugs [black people], builds bigger prisons, passes a three strike law and then wants us to sing 'God Bless America.' No, no, no, God damn America, that's in the Bible for killing innocent people," he said in a 2003 sermon. "God damn America for treating our citizens as less than human. God damn America for as long as she acts like she is God and she is supreme."

Yes, Mr. Obama sat through sermons like these for TWENTY YEARS prior to becoming president. Mr. Obama finally denounced him a few months after taking office, but that poses a question to me: "Why did he wait so long?" Mr. Jeremiah Wright has never changed his stance or speaking style, so what changed? Simple. Mr. Obama's desire to cut ties to the ugly truth. In fact, even after denouncing the inflammatory Wright, Mr. Obama, on Easter of 2011, attended a new church under new direction. New direction yes, but nothing new about the racist, Constitution hating ideology. This new pastor's name is Wallace Charles Smith. Mr. Obama and his wife attended an Easter Sunday service at Mr. Smith's church, Shiloh Baptist. In January of 2010, Mr. W. C. Smith was interviewed on ***the Jesse Lee Peterson Radio Show*** in which he said:

"Racism is still America's dirty little secret. The majority of Americans, unfortunately, are just about as leery of race and as fearful of race as ever. And I think there's a hostility, it may be underground, but it's still there."

"Racism is a one way street...blacks really can't be racist...racism implies you've got the power to enforce your prejudice and black people don't have the power to enforce their prejudice."

So, what is the truth, Mr. Obama? Are you against Water boarding? Or are you only against it if it isn't giving you brownie points with the people? Do you refuse to use signing statements because they give too much power to one man? Or are they only bad until the government refuses to continue funding your cronies? Are you a Christian? Or are you something totally different? Mr. President...who are you? Do you even know for yourself? The truth is, America, that President Obama's entire life and moral mindset has been radicalized, and he not only is surrounding himself with these radicals, but he lives right by them in their ideology. President Obama, dare I say it, is a walking presidential Overton Window of un-American red flags. And it's high time that we met some of the people behind this administration's White House, or should I say RED house.

PART TWO: The Man, The Myth, The Marxists:

If you want to know how a child will act when they grow up, watch their parents. If you want to see how the future of a country will turn out, keep your eye on its leader. Mr. Barack Obama has had, and currently has, relationships with people who openly despise what the U.S. stands for, and who would like nothing more than to transform it into something different. People including Van Jones, who was one of Barack Obama's hand-picked advisors in 2009. Van Jones is a man who claims in his own words, to have become radicalized in the aftermath of the 1992 LA riots led by Rodney King.

Jones, in May of '92, was part of a "nonviolent" protest against the verdict of Rodney King's incarceration and sentencing. In an interview on the subject, Jones said, *"I was a rowdy nationalist on April 28, and then the verdicts came down on April 29. By August, I was a communist."* Law enforcement officers in the area were afraid that the protest could turn ugly, so they arrested a number of protesters, including Van Jones. He spent a short time in prison, before all the charges against him were dropped. However, when asked about his incarceration, he had this to say, *"I met all these young radical people of color. I mean really radical: communists and anarchists. And it was, like, 'This is what I need to be a part of.' I spent the next ten years of my life working with a lot of those people I met in jail, trying to be a revolutionary."*

After his swift release from incarceration, Jones moved to San Francisco in 1993, where he established the Bay Area Police Watch, which specialized in the slander of local law enforcement officers. This was Van Jones trying to revive the "cops are pigs" movement. In 1996 he founded the Ella Baker Center for Human Rights, which was an organization that specializes in attacking the American legal system with accusations of racism and discrimination. The Ella Baker Center was headed by Jones from 1996 to 2007, and since its foundation, it has received over $1 million dollars from "the Open Society Institute," founded by corrupt billionaire George Soros.

By this time, Jones openly devoted himself to being an avowed Marxist who hated law enforcement and capitalism for *"exploiting non white minorities worldwide."* Jones became a leading member of STORM: Standing Together to Organize a Revolutionary Movement, a Marxist group that was staffed by members of Jones' Ella Baker Center. In the year 2000, Van Jones campaigned heavily against California Proposition 21, which at the time, called for harsher punishment for more violent offenses. In 2002, Jones produced an album for the Ella Baker Center starring the work of a convicted cop-killer Abu Jamal, such as, *"The American way manufactured by white folk in office, by these rich men here to mock us. The United States; a piece of stolen land led by right-wing, war-hungry, oil thirsty ... and when it's all said and done, still can't [garbled] the wrong place cause they got people of color playing servant to do that sh** for them; mother f***ers ready to wipe out soft targets on territories harboring terrorists? Tragedy. The true terrorists are made in the U.S."* Jones had fought against the incarceration of Jamal after he had been convicted and proven guilty of the grotesque murder of a law enforcement officer.

After his fizzled out "Anti-Prop 21 movement," Jones decided to change his campaign and political technique: *"Before, we would fight anybody, any time. No concession was good enough; we never said 'Thank you.' Now, I put the issues and constituencies first. I'll work with anybody, I'll fight anybody if it will push our issues forward.... I'm willing to forgo the cheap satisfaction of the radical pose for the deep satisfaction of radical ends."* On September 12, 2001, the night after the attack on the World Trade Center took place, Jones and other STORM members took part in a rally where Jones and STORM troopers gave a message to the U.S. claiming that we had brought this act of terror on ourselves.

Van Jones and STORM took part in a vast amount of anti war protests organized by another group of Jones' – International ANSWER – a group fronting the Marxist WWP: Workers of the World Party. On October 26, 2004, Van Jones took part in signing "the 9/11 Truth Statement," which called for the investigation into the accusation of President George W. Bush's involvement in the WTC attacks. As of September 10, 2009, Jones' name has been removed upon his request.

During the Bush Administration, Jones mocked President Bush on a number of issues; environmental in particular. "*We began to drill more, to drill off shore, to drill here, to drill there, to liquify coal ... to do whatever you can to get more petroleum into the system. And we heard our president saying just that. That's what he wants to do. And I hate to say this and I hope I don't offend anybody, but the president of the United States sounded like a crackhead when he said that. Just a little bit mo,' just a little bit mo,' a little mo', a little mo', a little mo' ... Like a crack head trying to lick the crack pipe for a fix ... I'm sorry, I'm gonna speak some Ebonics up here. Good luck with the translation.*"

Mr. Jones also co-founded "The Color of Change," whose goal was to pin the United States of America as a fundamentally racist nation. In 2005, CoC ran a campaign calling, again, for George W. Bush's reprimand, this time for Hurricane Katrina. In ***the Huffington Post***, Jones blames Katrina on President Bush's environmental policies.

At the end of the Bush Administration, Jones campaigned heavily for Barack Obama. On February 11, 2009, at a meeting where he was speaking, Jones was asked by an audience member why Bush was able to pass so much legislation when the republicans had only 60 senators in the house during his second term. Jones responded with, "*Well,* *the answer to that is, they're a**holes. That's a technical political term. And Barack Obama's not an a**hole. Um, now, I will say this: I can be an a**hole. And some of us who are not Barack Hussein Obama are going to have to start getting a little bit uppity."*

Wasn't that just sweet? Well, President Obama seems to think so. Despite Jones' rocky, ridiculous past, and his own words, on March 10, 2009, Barack Obama named Van Jones, "*Special Advisor for Green Jobs, Enterprise, and Innovation.*" Which I find funny, because in an interview in July of 2009, Jones was asked to describe a "green job" and its purpose. Here was his "response": "*Well, we still don't have a unified definition, and that's not unusual in a democracy. -It takes a while for all the states and the federal government to come to some agreement. But the Department of Labor is working on it very diligently. Fundamentally, it's getting there, but we haven't crossed the finish line yet.*"

Hmmmn ... did I say response? Sorry, I meant to say cop out. Regardless, because of "controversy" revolving around his atavistic and violent past, Jones resigned from the White House in 2009, and when requested, rejoined and is currently working for CAP: the Center for American Progress, a Group known for its influence in the Obama Administration and for its progressive roots. Coincidence? You tell me. In February of 2010, which is the same month Jones rejoined CAP, he received the NAACP's President Award, for his "*achievement in public service.*" This is only an example of one of the radicals that infest Mr. Obama's inner circle, and believe it or not, Van Jones isn't even the most stunning example.

WHITE HOUSE RADICALS:

Rahm Emanuel–Chief of Staff: Emanuel is known for his bare-knuckle politics. He has shown that he believes that the best way to get things done is to step on toes, bend the rules, and threaten whoever stands in your way. He once said, *"You don't ever want a crisis to go to waste. It's an opportunity to do things that you would otherwise avoid."* Mr. Emanuel lays his conscience down on the far left. According to Robert Knight's ***Radical Rulers***, his voting record concurs as he has consistently voted NO on banning partial birth abortions, NO on barring transporting minors into other states for abortions, and NO on making it illegal to harm a fetus during another crime. Emanuel is publicly and loudly profane, and has been since he worked for the Clinton administration.

Kevin Jennings–safe-schools Czar: Where to begin? This man is the last person I would want defending the safety of my kid in the school-place atmosphere. His stances on political reform and expanding a safer environment have absolutely nothing to do with school safety and everything to do with leftist radical progressivism. Jennings is a former schoolteacher and the founder of the organization GLSEN (Gay Lesbian and Straight Education Network), and I doubt that he put the term "straight" last because he wanted the acronym to sound nicer. In March of 2000, Jennings at a church conference said this to Christians: *"We have to stop being afraid of the religious right. We also have to quit … I'm trying to find a way to say this. I'm trying not to say 'f*** them!' which is what I want to say, because I don't care what they think! Drop dead!"* The conference where he was speaking was entitled, "Teaching Respect for All." This man does not support gay rights. He PUSHES gay supremacy in

America. In his book ***Becoming Visible***, Jennings posts the following questionnaire in the organization notes which has also appeared in schools across the country:

1. What do you think caused your heterosexuality?

2. When and how did you first decide you were heterosexual?

3. Is it possible heterosexuality is a phase you will grow out of?

4. Is it possible you are heterosexual because you fear the same sex?

5. If you have never slept with someone of the same sex, how do you know you wouldn't prefer that? Is it possible you merely need a good gay experience?

6. To whom have you disclosed your heterosexuality? How did they react?

7. Heterosexuality isn't offensive as long as you leave others alone. Why, however, do so many heterosexuals try to seduce others into their orientation?

8. Most child molesters are heterosexual. Do you consider it safe to expose your children to heterosexuals? Heterosexual teachers particularly?

9. Why are heterosexuals so blatant, always making a spectacle of their heterosexuality? Why can't they just be who they are and not flaunt their sexuality by kissing

in public, wearing wedding rings, etc.?

10. How can you have a truly satisfying relationship with someone of the opposite sex, given the obvious physical and emotional differences?

11. Heterosexual marriage has total societal support, yet over half of all heterosexuals who marry this year will divorce. Why are there so few successful heterosexual relationships?

12. Given the problems heterosexuals face, would you want your children to be heterosexual? Would you consider aversion therapy to try to change them?

As a school counselor, Jennings was once approached by a male student who opened up to him about a sexual experience the student had had in a bus station with a much older man. His advice to the student was *"You know, I hope you knew to use a condom."* Kevin Jennings is as radical as they come, and I pray that my generation does not have to suffer for it any more than they already have.

Cass Sunstein–Regulatory Czar: Long time friend and Chicago Law classmate of Mr. Obama, and one of the many progressive, tyrannical human embodiments in President Obama's circle. Mr. Sunstein, in 1992, expressed his firm belief that the President should hold a higher authority than any other official, and the ever-so famous progressive belief that the U.S. Constitution is a document that should be evolved, over time with the time. Not that it should change, the way the people say it should: *"That's the policy recommendation and the conclusion that the Constitution is largely, not entirely, but largely irrelevant.*

Now, I say what I've said about the Constitutional matter with considerable regret. I wish it weren't so. The executive department's vision of the Constitution, with the president on top and the administration below, has elegance and simplicity and tremendous appeal. It would make much more sense, I submit, given our current situation, to have a Constitution in which the president is on top and administration is below. But that was not the founder's original conception. The Constitution does not speak in those terms. Because the conclusion that I've reached seems to me so unfortunate, I'm trying hard to figure out what can be done about it. One thing that perhaps can be done about it is to say, well, we shouldn't really be originalists about the meaning of the Constitution. Maybe Judge Bork had it wrong. Maybe we should think that the Constitution has a high degree of flexibility. Maybe it's a changing and living document. Now, under that conception of Constitutional interpretation, maybe we can have the ingredients of a new unitary executive idea." Mr. Sunstein co-authored a book entitled "***Nudge***," and this book shows off, to some extent, Mr. Sunstein's view of the American people. He views them as experiments. Things that can be manipulated to do what he wishes. This book says, "*The state owns the rights to body parts of people who are dead or in certain hopeless conditions, and it can remove their organs without asking anyone's permission.*" Sunstein also co-wrote "***Animal Rights***": "*Animals should be permitted to bring suit, with human beings as their representatives, to prevent violations of current law.*" Speaking of which, I'm wondering when I'm gonna receive that court order from that family of squirrels whose relative I probably ran over. He also once wrote this in a book called, "***The Second Bill of Rights.***": "*Much of the time, the United States seems to have embraced a confused and pernicious form of individualism. This* *approach endorses rights of private property and freedom of contract, and respects political liberty, but claims to distrust 'government intervention,' and insists that people must fend for themselves. This form of so-called individualism is incoherent, a tangle of confusions."* Do I really have to say anything else about this man?

Mark Lloyd–Diversity Czar: A radical Un-American leftist who also follows the preaching of Saul Alinsky as he presses for drastic change of the first Amendment. He is notorious for attempting to shut down right wing radio stations, as he believes they control too much of the media empire. Well, someone obviously missed the '08 election. Mr. Lloyd's ideals and regulations would replace the voice of regular working class citizens with radical organizers. Mr. Lloyd once defined his belief of the first amendment: *"It should be clear by now that my focus here is not freedom of speech or the press. This freedom is all too often an exaggeration."* Lloyd also works at the Center of American Progress with his special buddy, Van Jones.

Carol Browner–Former Climate Czar: A known member of Socialist International, which is a group that attacks U.S. Policy - up until President Obama sanctioned her as his global warming czar. She was also among a list of fourteen leaders for Commission for a Sustainable World Society, which leans heavily toward Globalism and the idea that "Climate change" needs to be this new government's top priority. When she began work for Mr. Obama's administration, her name was removed from Socialist International's website, but there is a video clip of her speaking on behalf of the group in Greece. She worked for Mr. Obama until her decision to go home to feather her nest, where all radical progressives go: Back to the Center of American Progress with good ol' Vanny.

John Holdren–Science Czar: Mr. Obama's science and environmental advisor. In 1977, Holdren wrote a book that proposed the idea of population control by inserting birth control sterilants into a population's drinking water. Holdren and his co-authors treat the idea as a serious political proposal. Holdren is an ideological environmentalist who once wrote a post in ***the New York Times***, called, "***Convincing the Skeptics***": "*The extent of unfounded skepticism about the disruption of global climate by human-produced greenhouse gases is not just regrettable, it is dangerous. It has delayed - and continues to delay - the development of the political consensus that will be needed if society is to embrace remedies commensurate with the challenge.*" Holdren spreads the scare tactics of Al Gore when it comes to the "irrefutable" idea of man-made global warmi-err, I mean global COOL-err, I mean "climate change," as they have recently ruled even though many scientists have already dismissed the idea.

Harold Koh–State Department Legal Adviser: A long-time advocate of the shut- down of Guantanamo Bay, a detention facility that houses foreign criminals and terrorists of the United States. Koh believes that along with the shut-down, we should also give said foreign criminals, including Al-Qaeda terrorists, the right to trial in federal court. He claims in his own words that his goal is to see international law intervene with American law. He once wrote "*Domestic courts must play a key role in coordinating U.S. domestic constitutional rules with rules of foreign and international law, not simply to promote American aims, but to advance the broader development of a well-functioning international judicial system.*"

President Obama also has relations with All-American monsters, Bill Ayers and Bernadine Dohrn. These two were leaders of the 60's and 70's communistic terrorist group known as "Weatherman." They and their cohorts made law enforcement offices, military bases, even the Capitol Building, and Pentagon the targets of brutal bombings in the 70's. They were avid violent protestors against all things government, capitalism, and authority. They participated in "Weatherman's 1969 Days of Rage," in which they and other members of Weatherman enacted guerilla-style attack tactics to brutally wage violence against police officers, and civilians alike.

In 1995, Ayers formed the Chicago Annenberg Challenge or CAC, which aimed to achieve what Ayers saw as education's goal: "*... to teach against 'oppression'* ." How did Ayers view educational systems? Well I'll put it this way, he once wrote the foreword to a book by Mr. Kevin Jennings. Barack Obama was appointed by long time Chicago friend Ayers as the group's first chairman. Barack Obama and William Ayers worked side-by-side with each other for years. The CAC in its time has granted large amounts of money to other progressive groups such as ACORN: Association of Community Organizations for Reform Now, who strangely enough, contributed largely to Barack Obama's campaign and administration.

Bill Ayers, and his wife Dohrn, were monsters and rightfully pinned as such. They are terrorists to the United States of America, who have yet to denounce or appear remorseful, whatsoever, for their heinous crimes. They hate this nation, as Ayers claimed in an interview in 2001, "*What a country. It makes me want to puke.*" Here's something I found on Bill Ayers on informational site, www.discoverthenetworks.com. You tell me if you see something wrong with this picture:

- Leader of the 1960s and 70s domestic terrorist group Weatherman
- "Kill all the rich people ... Bring the revolution home. Kill your parents."
- Participated in the bombings of New York City Police Headquarters in 1970, of the Capitol building in 1971, and the Pentagon in 1972
- Currently a professor of education at the University of Illinois

Is it just me, or does this list make you feel like you're playing a game of "Which one doesn't belong?" This blew my mind. How, exactly, does this happen? How does a monster like Ayers become someone whose job is to be a leader for MY generation?

In his book *Fugitive Days*, which came to be in 2001, Ayers discusses his terrorist accounts, and refers to his attacks on the Pentagon, and Capitol Building: *"Everything was absolutely ideal ... The sky was blue. The birds were singing. And the bastards were finally going to get what was coming to them."* Ayers writes on to say, *"There's something about a good bomb ... Night after night, day after day, each majestic scene I witnessed was so terrible and so unexpected that no city would ever again stand innocently fixed in my mind. Big buildings and wide streets, cement and steel were no longer permanent. They, too, were fragile and destructible."*

He also writes that he would not rule out the possibility of resorting back to the use of bombs. Is that recent or serious enough for you? How about in December 2009, when Ayers and his wife actively participated in a violent anti-Israel protest in Egypt? The problem with twisted psychopaths like Ayers is that they actually believe that the things they do, are justified. That somehow, killing millions and millions of innocent people is going to change the way things are. Does that sound like someone who should be close to the President of the United States of America? An America-hating, blood-loving, murderous terrorist who has yet to denounce his actions? Its high time that the American people began taking the decisions of D.C. seriously and those decisions include who we allow into positions of power.

Part Three: Wake Up Call

I found an article in TIME magazine by Michael Kinsley called, ***Rejecting Obama's Radical Friends***. Kinsley begins by listing all of the horrible acts that Bill Ayers committed, and then goes on presenting the evidence of the relationship between Ayers and President Obama. Ayers threw a campaign party for the president in 2008. It sounds pretty sane so far, until I reach the line, *"Ayers and Dohrn are despicable, and yet making an issue of Obama's relationship with them is absurd."*

Mr. Kinsley also writes, *"Ayers and Dohrn never posed any real threat to U.S. national security. Their asinine chatter about killing people and their anti-American sloganeering were as ineffective as their bombs."* He finishes by saying, *"If Obama's relationship with Ayers, however tangential, exposes Obama as a radical himself, or at least as a man with terrible judgment, he shares that radicalism or terrible judgment with a comically respectable list of Chicagoans and others–including Republicans and conservatives–who have embraced Ayers and Dohrn as good company, good citizens, even experts on children's issues."* Well I hate to present myself as a non-conformist, but my take on Ayers, his wife, and anything they have been or are associated with should be considered nothing but a disgrace to this nation. In fact, they've just recently joined in the chaos in the middle east. They were spotted at an anti-Israel rally. And as far as them not being threats to security, they were single-handedly responsible for the bombings of major government and civil buildings, as well as for the deaths of thousands of innocent people.

Is it just me? Am I the only one who finds this dangerous idea of brushing off the president's friends and past, crazy? You cannot just dismiss relations between elected officials and radicals. The people that you surround yourself with have an impact on the way you believe and look at things, and those decisions shouldn't be brushed off, especially if you are the president of the United States of America. These are just two examples of people who President Obama has in his inner circle. I do not hate President Obama. I pray for blessings and wisdom upon him, his family, and his heart with the deepest sincerity. However, I will not give him a free pass just because he's the media's newest journalistic orgasm. If there are things in Mr. Obama's past that shouldn't be there, if he has openly said things falsely or changed his mind about them, if he is buddy-buddy with people who represent destructive ideals to my country, those are not characteristics I would allow a leader to have. It goes against everything sensible and sane.

Mr. Obama came in promising change and because we were so desperate to see it, we allowed him in with a staggering lack of credentials and credibility. There are plenty of others besides those listed that should not be where they are with the U.S. President, like Eric Holder, a U.S. Attorney general who has ties with the infamous 'Black Panthers' group- a flamingly violent black supremacist group that originated in the late 60's. Nancy Sutley, Chairman of Council on Environmental Equality who is a self advocated environmental activist who believes that the environment should have the same legal rights as humans. Sonia Sotomayor, Associate justice who pins the U.S. as racist and has ties to the racist Hispanic civil rights organization 'La Raza.' David Hamilton, U.S. District Judge who is a former ACORN contributor and current ACLU member. Timothy Geithner, Secretary of Treasury who sparked the banking investment crisis with his 'Bear Stearns' bailout. Janet Napolitano, Secretary of homeland security who wrote a report for the DHS after the '08 elections warning DHS Agents to brand anyone with a conservative bumper sticker as possible 'right-wing extremists' and threats to national security. George Soros, four-time White house visiting, dangerous globalist who hates capitalism and the U.S. dollar and is infamous for being a resounding denominating factor when economies collapse. In fact he is known as the man who broke the bank of England and once wrote in his book *The Age of Fallibility* that *"the main obstacle to a stable and just world order is the United States."* I could list and research all day, but the simple truth is that people in the President's inner circle are looking for a revolution of transformation. Ideals set forth for us in 1776 are being intentionally distorted today all over the map, and my generation is getting a large portion of the brunt of it.

In the 70's, Ayers told the youth to *"kill their parents."* Today, he, along with Van Jones and his organizations, tell youth to TEACH their parents with their "SHIFT THE POWER" movement. "Don't trust anyone over thirty kids, unless its one of us." Unless its union thugs who like to boo, flip the bird, and scream *"Fascist F**ks"* along with plenty more at the sound of America's national anthem. Let me tell you something America. The only reason I am able to tell you any of this is because my PARENTS and adults in my life who stand by real morals taught me how to also stand the correct way. I'm still learning from them and from life, the correct way to live because I am not anywhere close to knowing everything. I NEED the guidance of true American heroes. Not Union thugs, or presidential green-peace freaks, but real American citizens who know what it takes to make it.

I'm here to tell you that the real answer doesn't lie in transformation of this nation. It lies in the restoration of what we were originally built on. The outcome of our country cannot lie in the hands of these people. If we stand by our power as Americans. President Obama has openly said on more than one account that he plans to transform America. But at what costs? If it follows the path that we are on at the moment, then America 2.0 looks even scarier than Jon Stewart's haircut. The United states of huh? looks like a nation that is controlled by tyrants, with no sense of empathy for citizens. A nation no longer founded in principle, but in the drive for excess of materialism, or a nation where the only god that exists, is the one behind a microphone wearing a tie. America, our nation, as you read my words right now, is being transformed by radicals and it's nearly too late. Its HIGH time for us to wake up and stand up for the nation that is slowly being ripped out from under us. If we don't we WILL lose what we know and love. And what is put in its place, I promise, will only result in the suffering of generations to come. Wake up and take a lawful, peaceful stand. Use the tools that God granted to you at birth: Intelligence, Integrity, and your voice. Question everything that comes from Washington. The President of the United States is a role that should not be taken lightly by anyone. Not by the presidents and not by the people they lead.

There are too many dangerous and corrupt people in

power. It's up to you. Stand up for morality and honor as our founders did. Disavow anyone calling for violence, because we can't win back this country by inciting it. We win battles by being valiant, and smart. Use your brain and follow your heart. Do research and enlighten yourself with the whole truth. The Boston Tea Party in 1773 was the ignition to the American Revolution. It was an event that helped spark the movement toward a more perfect nation, and it wasn't incited by leaders, or by violent vitriolic radicals. The Tea Party of 1773 was lead by people who refused to take tyranny and unrepresented taxation lying down. America was coined when a group of ordinary citizens decided to fight toward something extraordinary in the name of freedom. Not by violence, hate, bloodshed, or dismantling of power, but by what they knew was right in their heart.

When it comes to the leader of a nation, it is an aspect that could break us, or make us. If that leader is surrounded by radical people shouting hatred, bloodshed, or unsupported accusation, it is up to the common sense and valiance of the people to make sure that the end result is the latter.

God has mapped out the path for America to follow. We just have to choose to take it, and not follow these radicals' path of folly. The bill for health care reform is three thousand pages long, while the Constitution only fills up four pages of parchment paper. The Constitution is a document that maps out our rights as human beings, and as Americans. The Constitution was written small because the government was meant to be small. The founders knew that to keep alive the country they created, the people of that country had to choose to keep it alive. Our country right now is in a downward spiral and history shows us that when that happens, people start taking sides. There are only two sides available for you to occupy: Good and evil. What side will you choose to stand by? Evil is growing at an alarming rate and the world we have all grown to know is on fire; a fire that was set by evil that no longer has any fear of showing itself. The world is splitting up, and the only way to put out this blaze is by choosing the right side, and by showing the evil, rearing it's head, that good is growing as well and it will not lose the battle.

Today, we are rejecting good all over the place. As of right now people are revolting, and they're doing it in ways that involve violence and vitriol. Some media pundits, even the president himself, are cheering for revolution. Cornerstones of our nation, including our faith, are being tattered by a society no longer afraid of God and openly hostile to Him. Even though there are plenty, I didn't have to look far for an example of this. All I had to do was type "*Christianity is*" into the Google search bar. Here's what popped up on the quick-search:

- *Christianity is bulls****
- *Christianity is a lie*
- *Christianity is a cult*
- *Christianity is false*
- *Christianity is not a religion*
- *Christianity is a joke*
- *Christianity is a straitjacket*

Our country and its principles are tearing apart at the seams. But do not lose hope, because we can still save it. All you need to do is find the good and stand by it. Choose to be on the side of principle and you are already doing half the job, but you have to first make the choice. Do you choose to follow the orders of a radical who tells you that you aren't smart enough to make something of yourself, or will you choose to plant yourself in the morals and ethics that you know lie inside you?

Will you be someone who chooses to do the right thing, and speak boldly on behalf of the generation following, or will you leave America to be reformatted from the inside into the structure of something that could very well ensure the suffering of generations to come? America truly is the last best hope of the earth. Will you be one who will remember the past, and fight to keep it that way or will you let that hope slip away? The choice is up to you America: Restoration or transformation?

Afterword

In 1776, Thomas Paine penned a series of writings entitled ***the Crisis Papers***, which included his famous work, ***Common Sense***. Paine's work sparked a revolution that birthed what would be known as one of the world's most prosperous nations. That nation was able to overcome all odds, and over time, has grown, encountering new economic, military, and moral issues. People have come and gone, rules have been revised, and mistakes have been made. But, the overcoming spirit of this nation is still alive and well somewhere. During the course of writing this book, I have been through a lot myself, and it hasn't been an easy ride. However, it's because of everything I went through during the course of this work that I know it's going places.

Paine's work did spark the movement for America, but only when the people decided to awaken the morality and strength of the human spirit that lay dormant inside them. Just like ***Common Sense***, this writing has the ability to spark an American revolution, if the people are willing to wake up the spirit. This revolution is not calling for a war, or the forming of a new government, it's a revolution calling for our restoration as a nation of hope. This rescue plan calls for the people to take their rightful place back from government under the laws previously set forth. Not by violence, not by blood, not by hate, but by principles and ethics that we are founded on as human beings.

As you can see, this country isn't founded on stimulus, or economics. Those are just leaves on our tree. Our country is rooted in humanity, and the principles that branch out from our roots, are the answers to solving any problem we may face as the people of the nation. The answers to rekindling our faith or morale in the United States, lies in the courage to be the individual you know you should be. Throughout the journey I've taken in writing this, I lost a loved one who taught me a lot, I had my heart broken, I've fallen and gotten back up, I've encountered new emotions, some good and some bad. Through this journey, all my answers were right in front of me. I didn't have to look too far for the right words to say, because they were in the lessons I was living out every day.

There are thousands of cycles that control today's society. The cycle of morale for an individual depends on the type day you're having. If you're having a good day, morale is at an all time high, and you feel like you can do anything you set your mind to. If you're having a bad day, you tend to slump around and lose faith a lot faster. The same goes for America, but the great thing about America is that in this country, cycles can be broken. We know that just one bad day doesn't mean the rest of our lives are going to turn out that way. Only we allow that to happen. If you let one bad day ruin the rest of your week, that's on you because it doesn't have to be that way. Think of the problems we face right now as just a bad day, because the dark times can and will end if we choose to make it happen.

There are things of this world that we cannot control, but there are also plenty of things that we can. The last four letters in the word *AMERICAN* are *I - CAN.* YOU are where the power lies. 'Yes we can' is good and it is imperative that we band together as a nation, but Yes WE can has to first begin with people who are willing to say, "yes I can." All you need to do is use what you have to the best of your ability. Don't you dare give in to the idea that you cannot change things because you are only one person. History is full of people who were willing to step forth and fight for their beliefs, and won. In this country we have rights, and freedoms, so let's use them, responsibly, and respectfully. No trampling on anyone else, no violent overthrowing of government, just fixing everything back to the way it's supposed to be. That's all it takes. Its time to enact a new revolution: a revolution in which people are led, not by violence, government, materialism, or aspirations of reform, but by morals, enlightenment, and common sense. People of America, in these last few pages, I want to challenge you to abide by the same principles set forth for us in 1776, by men who wanted to break away from tyranny and set up a nation founded by morality.

I challenge you to remember the past, and use it to your advantage. I challenge you to stand up for the faith founded in this country, and respect what we were built on. I challenge you to re-establish this nation as the beacon of light in the dark world that it once was. I challenge you to chase your American dream, and live by it with the principles of a true hero. I challenge you to accept all but those who pave their paths with violence, and present this nation united against them. I challenge you to question EVERY single bit of information that is handed to you, and to treat the media as if it were a hostile witness and do your own research. I challenge you to speak with boldness and responsibility and enlightenment. I challenge you to be someone who is willing to work for their happiness, and who recognizes the government as an aide, and not a lifestyle. I challenge you to be someone who holds strong when everything around you comes apart. I challenge you to love with your heart, and think with your brain. I challenge you to reach out to someone from a different generation. I challenge you to research who you are electing into office and make sure that no one is put behind the desk of the White House who is not based correctly in principle.

Lastly America, I challenge you to wake up your faith in our nation. Just because we have a few bad days, does not mean that we are finished, it just means we‘ve scraped our knees up a little bit, but America still has PLENTY of fight left in her. In 1776, we, as just 13 colonies, were able to stand up against the entire British regime, and form a whole new government. Since then, we have been brought in and out of countless hardships that we were able to move past because of who we are. That spirit of strength is still alive. It's in our schools, our homes, and our children. We just have to be willing to find it. You have the power. You are where the answer lies.

I'm not the only one who should be standing for this because we ALL have the ability to do so. Whether your contribution is a conference, a club, a book, or anything, do not burn out the fire of passion that's blazing inside of you. Do not stop fighting. Stand up, with peace, and love in your heart, and, with enlightenment as your source, keep fighting. Like Martin Luther King Jr., like the founders, like Americans, keep fighting. Some are asking is there still hope for America? Yes, and that hope is in you. Choose to stand by morality for your nation, and I promise you, its future is secure. God bless our future, the President, your decisions, your home, and your family. God bless America.

I Pledge Allegiance
To the Flag
Of the United States of America
And to the Republic
For which it stands
One Nation, Under God, Indivisible
With liberty and justice for all

Sources

Inform Yourself...

Chapter 1:

(1) "*The Charters of Freedom: A New world is at Hand*" The Declaration of Independence: A History http://www.archives.gov/exhibits/charters/declaration_history.html

(2) McDougal Littell "*The Americans*" by Gerald A. Danzer, Mcdougal Little 2003

(3) "*The Navigation Acts*" www.usahistory.info http://www.usahistory.info/colonial/Navigation-Acts.html

(4) "*The United States Declaration of Independence*" Thomas Jefferson 1776

(5) "*Constitution of the United States*" by Thomas Jefferson 1776 www.ushistory.org http://www.ushistory.org/documents/constitution.htm

(6) "*Under God*" by DC Talk's Toby Mac and Michael Tait Bethany House Publications 2004

Chapter 2:

(1) "*America's God and Country*" by William J. Federer Amerisearch, Inc. 1994- Literary Collections

(2) "*America's Providential History*" by Mark A. Beliles and Stephen K. Mcdowell Providence Foundation, 1991

(3) "*Constitution of Massachusetts*" by John Adams 1780 http://nhinet.org/ccs/docs/ma-1780.htm

(4) "*The Charters of Freedom: A New World is at Hand*" Constitution of the United States http://www.archives.gov/exhibits/charters/constitution.html

(5) "*First Prayer of Continental Congress, 1774*" Rev. Jacob Duche' September 7, 1774 http://chaplain.house.gov/archive/continental.html

(6) "*Jefferson's letter to the Danbury Baptists*" Thomas Jefferson January 1, 1802 http://www.loc.gov/loc/lcib/9806/danpre.html

(7) "*Common Sense*" by Thomas Paine published 1776 Penguin Books 2005

(8) CBN News Article CBNNews.com Thursday, August 19, 2010 "*Court Rules Against Utah Memorial Crosses*" http://www.cbn.com/cbnnews/us/2010/August/Appeals-Court-Rules-Against-Utah-Memorial-Crosses/

(9) "*It's Time to Update the Pledge*" David Waters Washington Post article December 1st, 2008 http://onfaith.washingtonpost.com/onfaith/undergod/2008/12/under_god_and_docherty_rip.html

(10) Letter from Thomas Jefferson to Dr. Thomas Cooper Feb. 10, 1814 http://www.stephenjaygould.org/ctrl/jefferson_cooper.html

Chapter 3:

(1) "*Immigration and U.S. History*" by Prof. Hasia Diner February 13, 2008 http://www.america.gov/st/peopleplace-english/2008/February/20080307112004ebyessedo0.1716272.html

(2) "*In Their Own Words: Reliving the Ellis Island Immigrant Experience*" by Juliana Smith Sept. 02, 2010 http://learn.ancestry.com/LearnMore/Article.aspx?id=15696

(3) "*History of the Statue of Liberty*" National Park Service http://www.statueofliberty.org/Statue_History.html

(4) "*American immigration Overview*" National Heritage Academies http://www.americanepic.org

(5) "*Statue of Liberty National Monument*" Emma Lazarus' "*The New Colossus*" http://www.libertystatepark.com/emma.htm

Chapter 4:

(1) "*The Glenn Beck Program*" Hosted by Glenn Beck aired December 14, 2010 guest: Jon Huntsman Sr.

(2) ABOUT US The Huntsman Corporation http://huntsman.com/eng/About_us/About_us/index.cfm?PageID=7383

(3) Walt Disney: A Short Biography by Brad A. http://www.justdisney.com/walt_disney/biography/w_bio_short.html

Chapter 5:

(1) Site of Skidmore, Owings & Merrill LLP http://www.som.com/content.cfm/one_world_trade_center

(2) "*Freedom Tower informational*" by Skidmore, Owings & Merrill LLP December 2003 http://www.renewnyc.com/plan_des_dev/wtc_site/new_design_plans/Freedom_Tower/freedom_tower_intro.asp

(3) "*LIFE: One Nation Remembers September 11, 2001*" by LIFE editors foreword by Mayor Rudolph W. Guiliani TIME Home Entertainment Inc. 2006

(4) "*Al-Qaeda (a.k.a al- Quaida, al-Qa'ida)*" by Jayshee Bajoria, Senior Staff Writer Greg Bruno http://www.cfr.org/publication/9126/alqueda_aka_alquailda.html

(5) Design by architect Michael Arad, and Landscape architect Peter Walker "*About the Memorial*" http://www.national911memorial.org/site/PageServer?pagename=New_Memorial_about

(6) www.ikhwanweb.com English website of the Muslim Brotherhood

(7) "*Islam: Governing Under Sharia*" by Toni Johnson & Lauren Vriens November 10, 2010 http://www.cfr.org/religion/islam-governing-under-sharia/p8034

(8) "Ikhwanophobia" by Pamela Taylor Monday, August 2, 2010 http://www.ikhwanweb.com/article.php?id=25890

(9) "*The 'Children Bombs' of Islamic Fundamentalists*" by Barry Dennis February 7, 2011 http://socyberty.com/issues/the-children-bombs-of-islamic-fundamentalists

(10) "*Children, Aged 5, used to plant Taliban Bombs in Afghanistan*" by Thomas Harding in Sangin June 30,2010 The Telegraph http://www.telegraph.co.uk/news/worldnews/asia/afghanistan/7863554/Children-aged-5-used-to-plant-Taliban-bombs-in-Afghanistan.html

(11) "*AIG offers first Takaful Homeowners Insurance Product for U.S.*" Article of Insurance Journal December 2, 2008 http://www.insurancejournal.com/news/national/2008/12/02/95930.htm

(12) "*Shariah finance watch has a list of Shariah Compliant Banks*" Article in Citizen Warrior http://www.citizenwarrior.com/2011/02/shariah-finance-watch-has-list-of.html

(13) Sharia-compliant Home-financing from Guidance Residential http://guidanceresidential.com/islamic-home-financing-sharia-compliant?gclid=CKyLld6snKgCFQprKgodgkY6JQ

(14) TheReligionofPeace.com Quran verses http://www.thereligionofpeace.com/Quran/023-violence.htm

(15) "*The Qur'an: Arabic Text and English Translation*" M. H. Shakir Tahrike Tarsile Qur'an, 1993

(17) "*Abortion Doctor Gunned Down at Kansas Church, Suspect in Custody*" Article at FoxNews.com May 31, 2009 Associated Press http://www.foxnews.com/story/0,2933,523581,00.html

Chapter 6:

(1) "*Arizona Shooting Victim Criticizes Palin, Beck, and Fox News*" by Joe Strupp January 14, 2011 http://mediamatters.org/blog/201101140044

(2) "*Mobilizing the Jobless*" by Frances Fox Piven December 22, 2010 http://www.thenation.com/article/157292/mobilizing-jobless

(3) "*Woodrow Wilson and White Supremacy: An Examination of Wilson's Racist and Antidemocratic Policies*" by Elvira Nieto June 20, 2009 http://www.suite101.com/content/woodrow-wilson-and-white-supremacy-a126787

(4) "*The Birth of a Nation and Black Protest: 'Art and History by Lightning Flash'*" Center of History and New Media http://chnm.gmu.edu/episodes/the-birth-of-a-nation-and-black-protest/

(5) Quote by Woodrow Wilson http://ffrl.wordpress.com/2010/10/28/quotable-my-presidency-is-ordained-by god/

(6) Quote by George Bernard Shaw in his speech on Humane Gas in 1934 http://www.atlassociety.org/tni/the-soviet-story-edvins-snore-communism-communist-chic

(7) "*Congressional Government: A Study in American Politics*" by Woodrow Wilson 1901

(8) "*Race Relations Under Theodore Roosevelt: The Brownsville Incident*" http://www.u-s-history.com/pages/h943.html

(9) "*Liberal Fascism: The Secret History of the American Left*" by Johan Goldberg 2007, 2009 Broadway Books

(10) "*The Overton Window: A Model of Policy Change*" by Joseph Lehman, Mackinac Center President http://www.mackinac.org/OvertonWindow

(11) "*Shooting Victim makes Death Threat*" *The Independent* January 17,2011 http://www.independent.co.uk/news/world/americas/shooting-victim-makes-death-threat-2186243.html

Chapter 7:

(1) "*History of the Frankfurt school*" http://frankfurtschool.us/history.htm

(2) "*Cultural Marxism*" by Linda Kimball February 15, 2007 http://www.americanthinker.com/2007/02/cultural_marxism.html

(3) "*An Inconvenient Book*" by Glenn Beck and Kevin Balfe Simon & Schuster, Inc. November 2007

(4) "*The Red Scare*" by Paul Burnett http://www.law.umkc.edu/faculty/projects/ftrials/SaccoV/redscare.html

(5) "*Armistice- End of WWI, 1918*" Eyewitness to History, 2004 http://www.eyewitnesshistory.com/armistice.htm

(6) http://www.cpusa.org

(7) "*Gregoire won't display gifted Nativity Scene Indoors*" by Brad Shannon, Staff writer of The News Tribune November 17, 2010 http://www.thenewstribune.com/2010/11/17/1427870/this-governor-wont-display-nativity.html#storylink=misearch

(8) http://www.facebook.com/cpusa Communist Party USA Group 6,360 members

(9) "*ACLU questions UI over marching Illini Chief*" by Paul Wood The News Gazette October 23, 2010 http://www.news-gazette.com/news/university-illinois/2010-10-23/aclu-questions-ui-over-marching-illini-chief.html

(10) "*Pro-Christian Chick-fil-A Targeted by Gay Rights Groups*" Article by Raven Clabough *New American* News Source February 7, 2011 http://www.thenewamerican.com/index.php/culture/family/6212-pro-christian-chick-fil-a-targeted-by-gay-rights-groups

(11) "*Feds admit storing checkpoint body scan images*" by Chief Political Correspondent of CNET DeClan McCullagh http://news.cnet.com/8301-31921_3-20012583-281.html

Chapter 8:

(1) U.S. National Debt Clock real time 2011 http://www.usdebtclock.org/index.html

(2) "*John Hansen, American Patriot and First President of the United States (1715-1783)*" http://www.marshallhall.org/hanson.html

(3) "*The Charters of Freedom: A New World is at hand*" The Constitution of the United States- A History http://www.archives.gov/exhibits/charters/constitution_history.html

(4) "*Read the bill Reality*" http://readthebill.org/?gclid=CJ_D-omU9aYCFcpU2godZSngAw

(5) Interview with Joseph Kenneth Clagett, Logistics Professional of CERE Project in 1994

(6) Editorial: "*No Obamacare for Obama*" by the Washington Times March 23, 2010 http://www.washingtontimes.com/news/2010/mar/23/obamacare-for-everyone-but-obama

(7) "*Margaret Sanger: Founder of Planned Parenthood IN HER OWN WORDS*" Diane S. Dew 2001 http://www.dianedew.com/sanger.htm

(8) "*Abstinence Programs Waste Taxpayer Money*" by Barry Raff, CEO Planned Parenthood of Hawaii, December 9, 2007 http://www.plannedparenthood.org/about-us/newsroom/local-press-releases/abstinence-programs-waste-taxpayer-money-21350.htm

(9) Article by Penny Starr CNS News November 11, 2010 http://www.cnsnews.com/news/article/planned-parenthood-got-3496-million-tax

(10) "*Alan Grayson (High Quality Version): Is Anyone Minding the Store at the Federal Reserve*" you tube video Representative Alan Grayson http://www.youtube.com/watch?v=cJqM2tFOxLQ

Chapter 10:

(1) Divorce Rate of the United States
http://www.divorcerate.org/

Chapter 11:

(1) "*ACLU Of Texas Protects Students' First Amendment Rights;*

Sweeny School Officials Must Change Unconstitutional Policy" http://www.aclutx.org/2011/04/14/aclu-of-texas-protects-students%E2%80%99-first-amendment-rights-sweeney-school-officials-must-change-unconstitutional-policy/

(2) "*Massachusetts School Issues Permission Slips for Pledge of Allegiance*" Article at Foxnews.com by Todd Starnes December 22, 2010 http://www.foxnews.com/us/2010/12/22/massachusetts-school-issues-permission-slips-pledge-allegiance/

(3) "*EXCLUSIVE: Teachers explain how they push Marxism in the classroom*" by Kyle Olsen Apr. 20, 2011 EAGtv http://www.eagtv.com/?p=203

(4) "*Parents Raging at Classroom Criminals*" article of New York Post by Erin Calebrese and Jennifer Fermino Apr. 26,2011 http://www.nypost.com/p/news/local/parents_raging_at_classroom_criminals_8SLQuIemOA08tYI3Yo8TcL

(5) "*Obama Zombies: How the Liberal Machine Brainwashed My Generation*" by Jason Mattera Threshold Editions, a division of Simon&Schuster Inc. 2010

(6) http://mariatalks.com

(8) http://www.barackobama.com/

(9)"*The 'Superman Controversy': What it's all about*" article of the Journal Sentinel by Jim Higgins May 2, 2011 http://www.jsonline.com/blogs/entertainment/121058978.html

(10) "*Statistics on Teen Drug Use*" http://www.teendrugabuse.us/teen_drug_use.html

(11) "*Teenage Depression Statistics*" http://www.teendepression.org/stats/teenage-depression-statistics/

(12) "*U.S. Teen Sexual Activity*" January 2005 Kaiser Family Foundation http://ww.kff.org/youthhivstds/upload/U-S-Teen-Sexual-Activity-Fact-Sheet.pdf

(13) "*Facts on American Teens' Sexual and Reproductive Health*" January 2011 Fact sheet http://www.guttmacher.org/pubs/FB-ATSRH.html

Chapter 12:

(1) "*Radical Rulers*" by Robert Knight Coral Ridge Ministries Media Inc. 2010

(2) "*Dreams of my Father*" by Barack Obama Crown Publishing, a division of Random House, Inc. 1994, 2004

(3) "*Obama's Communist Mentor*" by Cliff Kincaid February 18, 2008 Accuracy in Media article http://www.aim.org/aim-column/obamas-communist-mentor

(4) "*Explosive Undercover ACORN video!*" Thursday, September 10, 2009 http://atlasshrugs2000.typepad.com/atlas_shrugs/2009/09/explosive-undercover-acorn-video.html

(5) "*Obama Bans Waterboarding Terrorists, But Pentagon Won't Say If It Still Waterboards Military Trainees*" by Fred Lucas Tues. April 21, 2009 CNSNews http://www.cnsnews.com/node/46974

(6) "*CIA Chief: Water Boarding aided Bin Laden Raid*" article at MSNBC.com http://today.msnbc.msn.com/id/42880435/ns/today-today_news/t/cia-chief-waterboarding-aided-bin-laden-raid/

(7) "*Obama Signing Statement: Despite law, I can do what I want on czars*" article by Jonathan Strong The Daily Caller April 15, 2011 http://dailycaller.com/2011/04/15/obama-signing-statement-despite-law-i-can-do-what-i-want-on-czars/

(8) "*Americans United Commends Obama For Discontinuing Religious Right-Focused Prayer Event At White House*" article by Americans United for Separation of Church and State (AU) http://www.au.org/media/press-releases/archives/2009/05/au-commends-obama-for.html

(9) "*President Obama hosts dinner for Ramadan, Islamic Holy month, at White House*" article by the Associated Press September 2, 2009 NY Daily News http://articles.nydailynews.com/2009-09-02/news/17931697_1_islamic-holy-month-american-muslims-ramadan

(10) "*Obama's Pastor: God D*** America, U.S. to Blame for 9/11*" article by Brian Ross and Rehab El-Buri Mar. 13, 2008 ABC News http://abcnews.go.com/Blotter/DemocraticDebate/story?id=4443788&page=1

(11) "*White House Adviser Van Jones Resigns Amid Controversy over Past Activism*" by Scott Wilson and Garance Franke-Ruta *The Washington Post* September 6, 2009 htp://voices.washingtonpost.com/44/2009/09/06/van_jones_resigns

(12) "*Van Jones and his STORM troopers Denounced America the night after 9/11*" by Mattew Vadum *Canada Free Press* August 29, 2009 http://www.canadafreepress.com/index.php/article/14228

(13) "*Van Jones, Obama Adviser, Resigns Amid Controversy*"

by Will Lester *The Huffington Post* September 6, 2009 http://www.huffingtonpost.com/2009/09/06/van-jones-obama-advisor-r_n_278277.html

(14) "*Critics Assail Obama's 'Safe Schools Czar', Say He's the Wrong Man for the Job*" by Maxim Lott September 23, 2009 foxnews.com <http://www.foxnews.com/politics/2009/09/23/critics-assail-obamas-safe- schools-czar-say-hes-wrong-man-job/>

(15) "Obama's Science czar suggested compulsory abortion, sterilization" by David Freddoso July 14, 2009 washingtonexaminer.com http://washingtonexaminer.com/blogs/beltway-confidential/2009/07/obamas-science-czar-suggested-compulsory-abortion-sterilization

(16) "*Convincing the Skeptics*" by John P. Holdren *the New York Times* http://www.nytimes.com/2008/08/04/opinion/04iht-edholdren.1.14991915.html

(17) "*Scientists dismiss claims of runaway man-made global warming*" by Kirk Myers http://www.iceagenow.com/Scientists_dismiss_claims_of_runaway_man-made_global_warming.htm

(18) "*Obama Climate czar has socialist ties*" article by Stephen Dinan *The Washington Times* January 12, 2009 http://www.washingtontimes.com/news/2009/jan/12/obama-climate-czar-has-socialist-ties/

(19) "*Cass Sunstein*" Discover the Networks http://discoverthenetworks.org/individualProfile.asp?indid=2422

(20) "*Van Jones and his STORM troopers Denounced America the night after 9/11*" by Mattew Vadum *Canada Free Press* August 29, 2009 http://www.canadafreepress.com/index.php/

article/14228

(21) "*Van Jones, Obama Adviser, Resigns Amid Controversy*" by Will Lester *The Huffington Post* September 6, 2009 http://www.huffingtonpost.com/2009/09/06/van-jones-obama-advisor-r_n_278277.html

(22) "*Rejecting Obama's Radical Friends*" by Michael Kinsley May 29, 2008 TIME Magazine http://www.time.com/time/magazine/article/0,9171,1810338,00.html

(23) "*Bill Ayers*" Discover the Networks www.discoverthenetworks.org/individualprofile.asp?Indid=2169

(24) "*Obama: We'll 'Transform America'*" by Angela Galloway, P-I reporter December 12, 2007 *Seattle, PI Local* http://www.seattlepi.com/local/343184_obama12.html

(25) "*Reclaiming Revolution*" by STORM Spring 2004 http://www.leftspot.com/blog/files/doc/STORMSummation.pdf

(26) Van Jones http://vanjones.net/

(27) "*Van Jones*" Discover the Networks www.discoverthenetworks.org/individualprofile.asp?indid=2406

(28) "*9/11 Truth Statement*" Signatories Tuesday October 26, 2004 http://www.911truth.org/article.php?story=20041026093059633

(29) "*Controversial minister leaves Obama campaign : Presidential candidate condemns words but not ministry of former pastor*" Decision '08 Archive MSNBC.com http://www.msnbc.msn.com/id/23634881/ns/politics-decision_08/

(30) "*Content Warning Not Strong Enough for This Video of Leftist*

Freakout at Oregon Tea Party Rally" Scott Baker April 17, 2011 *The Blaze* http://www.theblaze.com/stories/content-warning-not-strong-enough-for-this-video-of-leftist-freakout-at-oregon-tea-party-rally/

Through darkest days
Through water's tide
Through good and bad
I'm on your side
I want you to know
I'll always believe in you…
-to Kenz

CPSIA information can be obtained at www.ICGtesting.com
Printed in the USA
244275LV00001B/2/P

9 780615 509679